WINNING EVANGELISM

(The Believer's Manual to Passionate Soul-Winning)

DR WILLIBROAD TICHA

DEDICATION

When the love of God in the hearts of many is becoming extinct, and people no longer see the need to identify with faith in God, there is still a remnant that not only has faith in God but is also fully committed to heralding His Good News to lost humanity, even when odds and persecutions mount up against them. To these few I dedicate this book as a source of encouragement. Seventy-five percent of the proceeds of this book will be used to sponsor evangelism and those who are dedicated to winning souls around the world.

ACKNOWLEDGMENT

I want to acknowledge all those joining my ministry across the nations through financial support, or collaborations in other ways to aid our evangelizing the lost.

FOREWORD

God is passionate for the souls of men. His heart is a burning fire for all of His creation. He is the same yesterday, today, and forever. He passionately desires that all men should come to repentance. You hold in your hands a book that speaks to that great passion. A book that will both instruct and inspire you to become a cutting-edge soul-winner. A book to equip you for the most exciting adventure of your life. Becoming a soul-winner is the most awesome call of every believer. You get to tell the greatest story ever told. My excitement about this book is because every concept and precept explained within its pages are all evidently portrayed in Dr Willibroad's daily lifestyle. So I can confidently affirm that what you will gather in its pages will not just be mere head knowledge as many are gifted in, but more so an impartation of spirit to make you become a contagious soul-winner.

May the Lord use this book to set your heart on fire for Him. I can't wait for the next best seller to be in book stores.

Apostle Dennis C. Moore
Founder/Director: Vision International Support Ministries
Senior Pastor of Churches
Sheriff & Hospital Chaplain

Contents

INTRODUCTION

The Christian faith is principally based on the life and ministry of Jesus Christ, the greatest gift God ever gave to mankind. Man was lost from the fall of Adam *(Gen 3)* and was cut off from the life of God and from fellowship with Him. Due to the fall, God worked out a redemptive plan for man, which was going to be through the crucifixion of the Son of God - Jesus Christ. And that through His sacrificial work on the cross, all those who believe and look up to Him will be saved.

This was accomplished and the atonement of sin through the spotless blood of Jesus Christ was realized. The door of salvation was eternally opened to all those who believe in Him to be the Son of God, and would allow Him be their Lord and Savior of their lives, as they confess Him to be so. Freedom from sin is achieved through His sacrificial blood on the cross. This door of salvation is opened to all who dare to believe, for the grace of God that brings salvation has appeared to all men, teaching us to denounce ungodliness and worldly lusts *(Titus 2:11-12).* If an individual will then respond positively, it will be because someone who is saved dared to take this good news of Jesus Christ to them.

Paul the apostle says he is not ashamed of the glorious gospel of Jesus Christ because it is the power to save the souls of men, irrespective of their cultural, and religious inclinations *(Rom 1:16-).* But the acceptance of the gospel also depends on how it is presented. Many have presented it poorly and have only met rejection and rebellion. Often it is not because the person is against the preaching of the gospel, but simply because it was presented in an unfriendly approach. The reverse is true if presented in a friendly and compelling approach.

To be sure that Christians fully understand what evangelism is all about, who to engage in evangelizing, the consequences of not evangelizing, as well as tips to be a successful soul-winner, is the reason this book has been written. I am very much excited about this book because ***it brings a twist on the subject that will tickle the innocence and the I –Already-Know-Mentality of every mind that reads it***. It will be my pleasure as you read this book, that you catch the fire for evangelism. See you on the mission field!

Yours in His Service,

WWT

Dr Willibroad Ticha

CHAPTER 1

THE GREATEST OF COMMISSIONS

Principe 1: Jesus is the Only Doorway to the father!

In Jesus's very own words, He said: *"...I am the way, the truth, and the life: no man cometh unto the Father, but by me."(Jn 14:6)*. This may seem offensive and may be considered as hate speech especially in the morally degraded and polluted society we find ourselves in today, which is filled with myriads of religions. A world where being politically correct means to compromise the truth to accommodate all kinds of philosophies and ideologies. Man, even Christian leaders have fallen for this deceitful scheme. Our concept of love for each other is anti-Christocentric. We have brought every other thing to the center of the circle while we keep Christ and His unswerving teachings on the periphery. Many in the fear of being side-lighted as fanatics have avoided the true message of the gospel as they become nothing short of comedians and motivational speakers.

I am so troubled because the quote of Jim Elliot, one of the missionaries killed by the Huaorani warriors on January 8, 1956, have become the fabric of modern-day Church - ***"We are so utterly ordinary, so commonplace, while we profess to know a Power the Twentieth Century does not reckon with. But we are "harmless," and therefore unharmed. We are spiritual pacifists, non-militants, conscientious objectors in this battle-to-the-death with principalities and powers in high places. Meekness must be had***

for contact with men, but brass, outspoken boldness is required to take part in the comradeship of the Cross. We are "sideliners" – coaching and criticizing the real wrestlers while content to sit by and leave the enemies of God unchallenged. The world cannot hate us; we are too much like its own. Oh, that God would make us dangerous!" [Ref: goodreads.com].

Once we come to the awareness that Jesus is the only doorway to the Father, and that the preaching of the gospel is the only invitation through which a person gets to Him, then our commitment to the preaching of the gospel of Jesus Christ will be more urgent. Paul the apostle says, ***"for I am not ashamed of the gospel of Jesus Christ, for it is the power of salvation unto all men"*** *(Rom 1:16).* And that his life will be in problems if he does not preach that Gospel *(1 Cor 9:16).* Preaching is still not enough, as we must measure our pace (our speed) on how we approach it - running the race while looking unto Jesus the author and perfecter of the faith *(Heb 12:1-2).*

Principle 2: God Does Nothing on the Earth Without Human Participation

This is a very important and dynamic principle, which if Christians understood, they will be strategically positioned for greatness of all sorts. *The heavens belong to the Lord, but the earth has He given to the sons of men (Ps 115:16).* Man is the only legal entity on the earth realm. Everything that needs to be done, whether of the Lord or of Satan, must involve human participation. God conveyed that authority to mankind from the time of his creation: "***And God said, Let us make man in our image, after our likeness: and let them have dominion over the... sea... air, and over... all the earth." Gen 1:26***

Man was given full authority over all the earth and over everything that is on the earth. So, for God or demons to accomplish anything over the earth realm, they need a man through whom they can be able to express themselves. Know that the Lord says, ***"I sought for a man that will build the hedge and stand in the gap" (Ezekiel 22:30).***

From the fall of man in the garden of Eden, God worked on the redemptive plan. He had to send the Savior, Christ Jesus, to die for the sins of mankind. But for Jesus to come into the world, God needed a man to bring that into realization. God said the seed of the woman will crush the head of the serpent *(Gen 3:15).* And when the fullness of the time for the fulfilment of this prophecy came, Jesus was born of the virgin Mary *(Gal 4:4).*

For the redemptive plan to be fully realized in the lives of people as God intends, there is the need for Christians to herald this message to the lost. Without their active role, humanity will be lost. Jesus commanded His disciples to pray the LORD of the harvest that He may send laborers to His vineyard. By this, He meant that the LORD God may send soul-winners.

The Great Commission Redefined

It is the formal and legal preaching of the gospel of Jesus Christ by a witness (disciple of Jesus Christ) to lost humanity, pointing the individual to the finished work of Christ on the cross, with the intention of bringing lost humanity into a restored fellowship with the Father and His Son Jesus Christ, through the Holy Spirit; thereby ascertaining of eternal life for that individual. Scripture is quite clear on this: ***"And this is life eternal, that they might know thee the only true God, and Jesus Christ, whom thou hast sent."***

(John 17:3) This fellowship is only made possible through the Holy Spirit, as He bears witness with our spirit that we are the children of God (Romans 8:16).

This is the greatest of commissions. Not just because it was given by the Lord Jesus Christ, but because:

i. It is the only legally approved way through which the redemption can be extended to the lost.

ii. It is the only one reason God got Himself involved in the diversity of ways in which He did in the different dispensations from the Fall of man to the present.

iii. It is the fulfilment of all that which the Prophets and the Laws pointed to.

iv. It is the one reason for which Jesus accepted to put on flesh and come die for lost man.

v. It is the only hope to be brought into the family of the Lord, and the sure guarantee of life with the Lord for eternity.

vi. It is the one reason the Holy Spirit relocated from heaven to the earth to abide with the Church and in the Church (the believer) for as long as the Church of Jesus Christ is still here on earth. Nothing else could be so important as to cause the Holy Spirit to relocate.

vii. It is the only commission with several mandates.

The Seven Mandates Within the Great Commission

Within the Great Commission, there are seven different mandates stipulated. If the revelation of these mandates is well apprehended by the believer, then the excellency of the results Jesus experienced in His life and ministry, will be experienced also by the believer. Just as Jesus assured His disciples that greater things than He has done will they do *(Jn 14:12).*

By mandate, we mean an official order to carry out a policy or a course of action, regarded as given by a superior board to an approved individual. Each of these mandates is very necessary to the fulfilment of the bigger picture (the Great Commission), as delegated by the board chair (Jesus) who is fully backed by the members of the board (the Godhead). Failure to take note of these various mandates, will lessen the passion with which the Christian gravitates towards its accomplishment, and will also reduce the full backing of the divine. These mandates can be seen within one of the key Scriptures that talks of the Great Commission:

"Then Jesus came to them and said, 'All authority in heaven and on earth has been given to Me. Therefore, GO and make DISCIPLES of ALL NATIONS, BAPTIZING them in the name of the Father, and of the Son, and of the Holy Spirit, and TEACHING them to obey all that I have commanded you. And surely, I am with YOU (ALL OF HIS DISCIPLES) always, even to the end of the age." (Matt 28:18-20 BSB)

But considering the fact that Scriptures does not contradict itself, when we read what Jesus told the disciples in ***Acts 1:4-5(BSB), "And while they were gathered together, He commanded them: 'Do not leave Jerusalem, but wait for the gift the Father promised, which you have heard Me discuss. For John baptized with water, but in a few days you will be baptized with the Holy Spirit.'"***

This was fulfilled ten days later: ***"When the day of Pentecost came, they were all together in one place. Suddenly a sound like a mighty rushing wind came from heaven and filled the whole house where they were all sitting. They saw tongues like flames of fire that separated and came to rest on each of them. And they were all filled with the Holy Spirit and began to speak in other tongues as the Spirit enabled them." (Acts 2:1-4 BSB)***

One can immediately realize there is supposed to be the Holy Ghost and fire baptismal experience that must precede ***"Therefore GO"*** of Matt 28:19. The minister must first receive this experience from the Lord Jesus if he will be sustained amidst challenges and burnouts, and experience the supernatural accompanying him in all ramifications. But there are others unfortunately who do not believe in this experience as they relegate it saying it ended with the apostles. Well, that's their choice. They haven't sinned in saying so, but they will simply live life and do ministry without divine help. Peter told the crowd that mocked this experience on the day of Pentecost, to repent and be baptized for the forgiveness of their sins. Then, they will also receive this experience, emphasizing to them that the promise was not only for them (the apostles), but also to them that were present and their children, as many as the Lord will keep calling to salvation *(Acts 2:37).* This would mean if people still receive salvation today, then this experience also is supposed to be for them. Because most pastors today have not received this experience, they have not been able to train their spirits accurately to hear the voice of God. And in cases that they are supposed to know with precision what the LORD is saying, they have gone for votes to know what God wants. Some say, ***"I feel the Lord is telling me to..."*** Beloved, hearing the Holy Spirit is not a feeling, but a certainty. Paul emphasized to Timothy that *the Spirit now speaks clearly* (2 Tim 4:1).

A- The "Holy Ghost (Fire) Baptismal" Mandate

This is a very dynamic experience for the believer if the Great Commission will forcefully advance. This experience was clearly prophesied by two prophets of the Old Covenant, Joel and John the Baptist. Their prophecies were quite distinct with regards to this experience:

"...I will pour out My Spirit on all people. Your sons and daughters will prophesy, your old men will dream dreams, your young men will see visions. Even on my menservants and maidservants, I will pour out My Spirit in those days. I will show wonders in the heavens and on the earth..." Joel 2:28-30 BSB

"In those days John the Baptist came, preaching in the wilderness of Judea... This is he who was spoken through the prophet Isaiah: "A voice of one calling in the wilderness, 'Prepare the way of the Lord, make straight paths for Him.'" ...I baptize you with water for repentance, but after me will come One more powerful than I, whose sandals I am not worthy to carry. He will baptize you with the Holy Spirit and with fire. His winnowing fork is in His hand to clear the threshing floor and to gather His wheat into the barn; but He will burn up the chaff with unquenchable fire." Matt 3:1-12 BSB

Jesus Christ also emphasized the importance of it by insisting that the disciples should not venture into going out with the mandate of the Great Commission without first of all seeking God and waiting for this experience:

"So when they had come together, they asked Him, "Lord, will You at this time restore the kingdom to Israel?" Jesus replied, "It is not for you to know times and seasons that the Father has fixed by His own authority. But you will receive power when the Holy Spirit comes upon you, and you will be My witnesses in Jerusalem, and in all Judea and Samaria, and to the ends of the earth."" Acts 1:6-8 BSB

Concerning the Great Commission and the fierce nature of it, very little can be done without this Fire Baptism. This is one of the few spiritual experiences that empowers the believer and exposes them to the realm of the supernatural.

When you take a keen look at the above scriptures concerning the Fire Baptism, you would immediately see that there is an aspect of judgement that accompanies those who go through this experience. It is a judgement that deals with the forces of wickedness against the advancement of the kingdom of God. John the Baptist emphasized that His winnowing fork is in His hand to clear His threshing floor and to gather His wheat into the barn, but He will burn up the chaff with unquenchable fire. This deals with severely judging the things that opposes the harvest. That is, the harvest of souls. This will involve coming against political laws instituted against the Church and against evangelization.

I remember planning g to travel to Comoro some years back for evangelization, when I was told that the president of Comoro passed an anti-conversion law, forbidding Christians from attempting to convert Muslims to Christianity. Though the Muslim population then was about 99% and the Christians about 1%. That is why we need believers who have these Fire Baptism experience in order to oppose and judge such state laws which are against the spread of the

Great Commission. For it is at the face of such oppositions that the supernatural acts of God are manifested. Like the case of King Nebuchadnezzar who opposed the children of God. God's judgement fell on him and he became like an animal living in the forest for seven years until he learned to know that the *Lord God rules in the affairs of men (Dan 4).*

Becoming a preacher and not having this experience is like a toothless bull dog that barks. It is like trying to use an ancient analog camera in the technological world of today. It is like driving an ancient Volkswagen through the heat of the Sahara as opposed to flying across it with a jet plane. This is an experience which the religious mind can never understand. They never understood it in the time of the disciples when the Holy Ghost came on them, and neither do they understand it today:

"And when the day of Pentecost was fully come, they were all with one accord in one place. And suddenly they came a sound from heaven as of a rushing mighty wind, and it filled all the house where they were sitting. And there appeared unto them cloven tongues like as of fire, and it sat upon each of them. And they were all filled with the Holy Ghost, and began to speak with other tongues, as the Spirit gave them utterance... The multitude came together, and were confounded...And they were all amazed, and were in doubt, saying one to another, What meaneth this? Others mocking said, These men are full(drunk) of new wine." Acts 2:1-13 KJV

The religious mind will always try to explain what they do not understand spiritually as drunkenness or madness. Mocking what they know nothing about. That is why many Christian denominations today have mocked churches that believe and practice this Holy Fire Baptism experience. In as much as the minister must ensure he has received this experience; he also must place a demand on the Lord to use him to bring many others to this fire experience. This is because the Holy Ghost Fire baptism is necessary for a supernatural walk. It is within the jurisdiction of this mandate that the individual begins to pray in the Spirit (in tongues), thereby edifying himself spiritually even when he is surrounded by challenges. This is because praying in the Spirit, is the Holy Spirit searching the deep things of God and making intercession for us through our spirit according to the will of God *(Rom 8:26-27),* and not our minds. As a result of His intercession, all things begin to work all together for our good (Rom 8:28). In fact, the mind is unfruitful during that moment *(1 Cor 14:14).* So, the mind does not understand what the spirit is saying, and neither is the spirit influenced by the thoughts of one's mind to determine what the utterance would be.

This experience sets up the spirit of the individual to an ever infilling experience irrespective of the surrounding challenges. This ever infilling of the spirit would otherwise not be possible if the individual was conscious of his circumstances. It is also as a result of this experience that the believer learns to exercise his spirit and train it to hear the voice of the Holy Spirit. Jude admonished us to constantly build ourselves on our most holy faith as we pray in the spirit *(3:20).* It is important to note that this most holy faith comes by meditating on the unadulterated word of God *(Rom 10:17).* As we meditate and pray, we receive revelations of His w builds up our spirits to the point that we are able to word, which builds us to discern the voice of God from the voice of evil: ***"For everyone who lives on milk is still an infant, inexperienced in the message of righteousness. But solid food is for the mature, who by constant***

use have trained their senses to distinguish good from evil." (Heb 5:13-14 BSB) Therefore principally two things activate our hearing capacity to the voice of the Holy Spirit - a constant meditation on the word of God for revelation truths, and praying in the spirit(tongues).

It is time Christian leaders realize that this experience is the first mandate revealed in the Great Commission, and it is what opens the spirit of the believer to pursue the other mandates of the commission.

B- THE "GO" MANDATE

This is the instruction for the disciples to engage into witnessing for Christ. It does not give any believer any other options from going. Jesus earlier told His disciples in ***Acts 1:8 (BSB), "But you will receive power when the Holy Spirit comes upon you, and you will be My witnesses in Jerusalem, and in all Judea and Samaria, and to the ends of the earth."***

The verb "GO" in the original manuscript (Koiné Greek) was constructed in the Greek in aorist participle. This verb construction does not really exist in the English language. This talks of an action that began in the past and keeps continuing to the future. A most literal translation of the word "GO" in the verse "Therefore, GO and make disciples..." would be; Therefore, HAVEN GONE, make disciples..." This is because evangelizing was not a new instruction Jesus was giving to His disciples. They had already began evangelizing. His emphasis here is in what to do haven gone evangelizing. Hence, the act to GO evangelize is IMPLICIT for the believer. Once a person is born again, witnessing for Jesus should become automatic and not something anyone should wait to be instructed. It is a revelation that needs to be taught to the young believer. Infact, waiting to be commanded to GO evangelize is disobedience to the Great Commission. Once this revelation about soul-winning gets whole of the believer, soul-winning will become a lifestyle. Looking at how Jesus presents this "GO" mandate, one can immediately see the urgency and the importance of it. This same urgency is demonstrated all across the scriptures. Paul says his life will be in problems if he does not preach the gospel *(1 Cor 9:16).* He also cautions his spiritual son, Timothy, to be ready to preach the gospel at all times, whether in season or out of season *(2 Tim 4:2).*

This would therefore imply that not to be prepared at all times to "GO" for the gospel is already acting contrary to the terms of the Great Commission. Peter in his first epistle admonishes us to this consciousness to take the gospel to the people when he said, ***"But sanctify the Lord God in your hearts: and be ready always to give an answer to every man that asketh you a reason of the hope that is in you..."(3:15 KJV)***

Be Highly Exalted Lord

By sanctify the Lord God in your heart as seen above, the Scripture means that God must be highly exalted in our hearts above all else, above all philosophies, and above all conspiracies. Nothing must be allowed to interfere with the Lord, nor with His precepts and concepts. David said to the Lord, that he has considered and esteemed all His precepts about all things to be correct, and that anything contrary is a false way and that he hates it *(Ps 119:128).* Paul in speaking to the Church in Ephesus about how highly Jesus has been exalted at the right hand of God the Father in heavenly places, said: ***"Far above all principality, and power, and might, and dominion, and every name that is named, not only in this world, but also in that which is to come: And hath put all things under his feet, and gave him to be the head over all things to the church, Which is his body, the fullness of him that filleth all in all." (Eph 1:21-23 KJV)***

If we can be conscious of the greatness of the Lord and He being highly exalted in our hearts above all powers, principalities, pleasures, etc., nothing will top us from declaring the good news about Him and all that He has done to save the lives of men. For the Church to reach appoint where every Christian is passionate to "GO" with the gospel to the lost, we need to bring them, through teaching of the word, to the revelation of the person of the Lord Jesus and His surpassing greatness. For when His person and greatness is being revealed, the passion to tell others about Him is automatic. This is what Jeremiah meant when he said the word of God was like fire shut within his bones, that there was no way he could stop telling people about the Lord, even when he decided not to make mention of the Lord again *(Jer 20:9).*

C- The Discipling Mandate

The discipling mandate defines the second phase of obedience by the minister with regards to the Great Commission. It focuses on establishing the newly converted souls into the faith. So that their walk with the Lord Jesus Christ can be progressive. This was the phase that Luke meant when he addressed his book to Theophilus: ***"Many have undertaken to compose an account of the things that have been fulfilled among us, just as they were handed down to us by the initial eyewitnesses and servants of the word. Therefore,***

having carefully investigated everything from the beginning, it seemed good also to me to write an orderly account for you, most excellent Theophilus, so that you may know the certainty of the things you have been taught." (Lk 1:1-4 BSB)

Taking a keen look on the purpose of Luke writing this book to Theophilus, there are a couple of lessons to glean from it, which will enhance our walk of faith and help us to fully and practically obey the various mandates within the Great Commission. Some of these lessons are:

(i)- Do not leave the responsibility of spreading the faith in the hands of others only.

Many had taken the responsibility of writing about the life and ministry of Jesus. One cannot tell the purpose why they were each doing so. It could be for historical, journalism, or business purposes. Since Jesus' ministry was quite spectacular and caught the attention of the entire nation, it was obvious that people would want to know more about Him and His ministry - whether they believe in Him or not. This motivated many writers to engage in writing about it. Others could have also been writing from a spiritual standpoint, whatever their purpose was. But most importantly, Luke took upon himself the responsibility to do a thorough research about His life and ministry, so as to present to Theophilus an orderly account which will be the basis of Theophilus faith in the things he has been taught about Jesus Christ. This therefore means that Luke's purpose for writing to Theophilus was for discipleship - so that he may know the certainty of the things he has believed. Luke took upon himself the responsibility to disciple Theophilus. We are not supposed to do less with regards to the people we reach the gospel with!

Considering how demanding it would be to do a thorough study about the life of Jesus, from the beginning of His days to the end, it would have been enough reason for Luke to shy away from such task. But one thing that was burning in his heart was the discipleship of Theophilus, so that he can be firmly established in the faith. This compelled Luke to engage his time and finances. He was compelled by the love of God and the love for Theophilus to be established in the faith much more than whether he felt he was called for that or not. Unfortunately, many have blushed away the desire to help disciple others under the pretext - it's not their calling. That's not true! The problem is not that they are not called (for all are called into that), but that they have not loved the Lord enough for Him to interrupt their private agendas for the Kingdom agenda. Jesus taught His disciples to always seek God's will to be done on the earth, and the coming of His Kingdom, every time they pray. Neither of these will be realized if the Church will not arise to take the initiative to reach out to the people.

(ii)- Careful studies of the scriptures

Discipleship is only going to yield the right results in the lives of the people if they are discipled according to the pure unadulterated doctrine of God's word. That is the only way their lives can be reflect the life of Christ. Paul admonished Timothy to study so as to show forth himself approved unto God, a workman that has no need to be ashamed, but who rightfully divides the word of truth *(2 Tim 2:15)*. Proper discipleship will dispel all doubts from the heart of the newly saved. Many do not understand basic biblical concepts; such as the Trinity, new birth, life after dead, etc., because they were not properly discipled ***[See my book (Found on Amazon.com bookstore): The Journey (Now That You Are Saved)].***

This places a strong demand on the minister to build himself in the true teachings of Jesus Christ. Unfortunately, many ministers have not taken upon themselves the responsibility to search the Scriptures thoroughly. Many do teach simply what they have been taught, without affirming the certainty of those things from a true unbiased biblical perspective. The saints of Berea were commended for the practice of searching the Scriptures daily to affirm the things that Paul had been teaching them *(Acts 17:11).* Irrespective of one's calling, we all as believers have to ensure we feed daily on the word of God to build ourselves on the true teachings of the word. This will make us effective disciple-makers in the faith.

(iii)- Nothing is too costly for the sake of a soul.

Nothing indeed is too costly for the sake of establishing an individual in the faith. If it needs you to drive for miles to where they are, or you spending some money in the process, do it! The Scriptures tells us if we are asked to go one mile, we should go two *(Matt 5:41).* Paul reiterated this when he said, ***"I did not shrink back from declaring anything that was helpful to you as I taught you publicly and from house to house..." (Acts 20:20 BSB).***

What makes discipleship very demanding at times is because one person is spiritually matured (the disciple-maker), while the other is spiritually immature (the one being discipled). So, it necessitates endurance, patience on the part of the disciple-maker. The Lord commands that the disciple-maker should patiently teach *(2 Tim 2:25).* It is never a comfortable experience, and that explains the reason why many Christians feel they have not been called into it. There will be much you would have to put up because of the person you are discipling.

What actually makes the process successful is not just what you teach them, but the example they see in and through your own life; the character you display when confronted by challenging situations, the attitude you put on when people look down on you. This is where the Pharisees were missing it, as Jesus rebuked them that they travel miles to win souls, then bring them to the synagogue and make them twice candidates for destruction *(Matt 23:15).* And the fact that they give heavy burdens to people to carry, meanwhile they themselves cannot carry such loads with their tiny finger *(Matt 23:4).* They were preaching what their lives were not exemplifying and as such, contaminating the lives of the people more. In fact, if a new convert will continue in the faith in the long run, and be able to endure whatever come his way without denouncing the faith, it will be determined by how well he was discipled.

Hit and Run

This is when you reach an individual with the gospel, then they get saved, then the preacher departs and never follows up. If something can be done to ensure a follow-up, then it will be great to go for it! It is true that often, especially with the schedule of either the preacher or the one evangelized, meeting again may be difficult. They might have met at the airport, roadside, without no hope of ever meeting again. What the evangelist could do is to get the contact information of the individual if they will be willing to give it. Then to reach out on phone, social media, or through any other available means. It would be beneficial to refer the individual to a living church in his area.

Effective evangelism is not completed without strategies being put in place for the continual discipleship of the individual

In order to avoid ***hit and run***, it is important for the evangelist to have a network of individuals (churches) that can always work with him towards the discipleship of souls. No matter how hard it may be, all efforts must be done for the continual discipleship of the newly saved. For that is mandated by Jesus Christ in the Great Commission. This would mean.

Effective evangelism is not completed without strategies being put in place for the continual discipleship of the individual. Often, when discipleship is not carried with someone who newly got saved, even if the person does not end up backsliding, he may suffer certain things due to ignorance of the Scriptures that could have been avoided had he been discipled. In case you have done all but can't maintain contact with the individual, then do what Paul the apostle did when he said, ***"And now, brethren, I commend you to God, and to the word of his grace, which is able to build you up, and to give you an inheritance among all them that are sanctified." (Acts 20:32 KJV).*** Pray and commit the individual to God, for He will know how to keep the individual in the faith. For the seed has been planted.

D- The Cultural Mandate

This is the mandate that ensures that the gospel of Jesus Christ goes to every ethnic group of the world. Reaching out to every ethnic group with the gospel has been the divine plan and agenda. Abraham called of God to be the father of faith was not only for the

Hebrew children, but for every nation of the world - ***"And through your offspring all the nations of the earth will be blessed, because you have obeyed My voice." (Gen 22:18 KJV).*** This was a word of promise of salvation through Abraham to every nation (ethnic group) of the world. Jesus laid emphasis on this when He said we should make disciples of the nations *(Matt 28:19).* The Greek word here for nations is *"ethnos,"* which means ethnic. This is a community or population made up of people who share a common cultural background or descent. They speak the same language.

The Cultural Mandate demonstrates the love of the Father for the people of every ethnic group without discrimination to culture or race. The gospel has to successfully go to every ethnic(cultural) group with evidence of disciples won from each of them before the end shall come *(Matt 24:14).* This is precisely what the cultural mandate is all about. Every leader must be conscious of this and should seize the opportunity to get the gospel to people of different ethnicity as much as they can. Even if they are not involved directly in doing that, they should support ministries that go cross-culturally.

Challenges of the cultural mandate

Cultural groups are very delicate to deal with, as people are very sensitive to whatever teachings may contradict their worldview about deity.

With this mandate, there are lots of challenges. First of all, a preacher or evangelist who has not been well trained, will find it very challenging in a cross-cultural setting. This is because he is dealing with people of a different ethnicity, which comes with difference in mindsets, perspectives, behaviors, religious views.

Often, cultural groups are very delicate to deal with, as people are very sensitive to whatever teachings may contradict their worldview about deity.

It requires the missionary evangelist to be well trained on how to approach people of different cultures in a way that will not be offensive. For this to be possible, the missionary evangelist needs to be flexible in his approach. Paul said he became all things to all men that by all means, he may win some *(1 Cor 9:22)*. This is the cultural mandate being engaged by Paul the apostle.

Be well trained on how to approach people of different cultures in a way that will not be offensive.

Depending on the different cultural environment Paul found himself in, his approach was accordingly. There are factors that the missionary evangelist must take note of if he must succeed in a different cultural setting. These are:

(i)- Patience is greatly needed

How long it will take to successfully penetrate a culture with the gospel will depend on the vastness of the difference in cultural beliefs from that of the missionary.

As he communicates the gospel, he must be very patient with the people. He has to exercise patience as he first of all builds a trustworthy relationship with the people. This is when they become comfortable to open their hearts to hear his teachings.

How long it will take to successfully penetrate a culture with the gospel will depend on the vastness of the difference in cultural beliefs from that of the missionary. The differences will make his mission more delicate, as he may face hostility from the indigenous he is trying to reach out to, if he does not know how to easily adapt.

Paul found himself in Ephesus, a hostile culture which was filled with idolatry. The people opposed Paul greatly, but he was so patient with them that he had to stay in that city for three years as he preached daily, reasoning with them the scriptures, before he finally had a breakthrough *(Acts 19:20).*

(ii)- Become Untraditional

A true evangelist must be untraditional. This has to do with adapting to new ways of doing the same things, and presenting the gospel. This is because you want to ensure your message can easily go through without you being seen as a stranger. This entails missiological training and principles. This calls for flexibility and adaptability; the ability to present your message in a way that will be understood and appreciated by the people of that ethnic group, without necessarily adopting certain elements within their culture which is anti-biblical perspective. This is what Paul meant by becoming all things to all men that by all means he might win some.

A true evangelist must be untraditional. This has to do with adapting to new ways of doing the same things, and presenting the gospel.

Any evangelist who cannot be flexible and untraditional, cannot be effective in fulfilling the Cultural Mandate.

Any evangelist who cannot be flexible and untraditional, cannot be effective in fulfilling the Cultural Mandate. That is the reason why so many leaders have not engaged into cross-cultural missions with the vision of their ministry. Even those who do engage find it difficult to succeed. This is because it takes much more than just understanding what soul-winning is about.

(iii)- Study and familiarize yourself with their beliefs

Time is needed for the missionary to familiarize himself with the traditional and religious beliefs of the people. This is because ministering to them, will involves dissolving certain beliefs they previously upheld. Until some of these beliefs have been dissolved, they will not realize nor appreciate the truth. Paul in Athens, studied and researched about all the altars of the Athenians before he approached them with his gospel. Knowing who they are, their beliefs, etc. prepared him on how to present the gospel message to them in ways that will encourage them to desire to know more about the truth *(Acts 17:16-34).*

The mistake most missionaries make is that they assume they already understand the cultures and traditions of the people they are approaching. Because of that, they fail to educate themselves on the rightful methodology of approaching them. This has resulted to the so many unsuccessful mission trips, as many have abandoned their mission field because they attracted unnecessary persecution due to lack of skillfulness as missionaries.

(iv)- Understand the art of cross-cultural presentation

The gospel must be presented tactfully and skillfully. Do not put on an attitude when the indigenes seem to challenge your teachings initially. Rather, be consistent on teaching the truth in a fashion that is exciting, appealing, and respectful.

In any way your teaching agrees with any of their practices or beliefs, identify with that. Make mention of that every now and then as you teach. It influences them psychologically to open their hearts to what you are preaching.

In any way your teaching agrees with any of their practices or beliefs, identify with that. Make mention of that every now and then as you teach. It influences them psychologically to open their hearts to what you are preaching. Paul while in Athens, saw the several altars (representing their various religious beliefs) of the Athenians and identified with the altar that was dedicated to the Unknown God. They gave him their undivided attention as he explained to them who this unknown God is all about. Though others mocked him, yet he persisted without getting into any fierce argument and some eventually got saved *(Acts 17:27-34).*

E- The Baptismal Mandate

Jesus commanded the disciples that as they go evangelizing, they must baptize those who accept their message and repent from their sins. Not many evangelists are conscious of this. The issue of baptism today has become more of a doctrinal issue within denominations. Though baptism is what almost every denomination believes in, yet they have differences with regards to the subject. Some of the differences are:

i. Who is qualified to be baptized?

ii. Is baptism mandated for salvation or it is just a symbolic act?

iii. Can children be baptized?

iv. Is eternal life guaranteed once a person is baptized?

There could be many more differences than are listed here. Some of the doctrinal differences is for the sake of order as some would consider it, but most of it is due to difference in perspectives with regards to baptism. Irrespective of the differences, it is important to understand the concept of baptism from the biblical perspective, and its significance for the believer.

What is water baptism and what purposes does it serve?

Baptism is an outward sign of an inner reality (regeneration). Here we identify with Christ's death, burial, and resurrection. Other names for this are baptism of repentance, and baptism by burial:

"Then Peter said unto them, Repent, and be baptized every one of you in the name of Jesus Christ for the remission of sins, and you shall receive the gift of the Holy Ghost." Acts 2:38

"Know ye not, that so many of us as were baptized into Jesus Christ were baptized into death? Therefore, we are buried with him by baptism into death; that like as Christ was raised up from the dead by the glory of the Father, even so we should walk in newness of life." Rom 6:3-4

> "When John had first preached before his coming the baptism of repentance to all" Acts 13:24.

John the Baptist was the first human preacher of water baptism:

"When John had first preached before his coming the baptism of repentance to all" Acts 13:24. He emphasized to those who were coming to hear the word he preached: ***"Repent ye for the kingdom***

of heaven is at hand... then went out to him Jerusalem... and were baptized of him in the Jordan, confessing their sins." Matt 3:2-6.

Scriptural mandate for water baptism (by immersion) is only after repentance from dead works. This therefore disqualifies the baptism of little children who are still in a state of innocence (not conscious of neither right nor wrong). Water baptism was done by immersion and not by sprinkling, as the case is with certain denominations. This is because the word "baptize" was derived from the Greek "baptidzo," which was used by the Jew to describe a ship that sinks into water, or a person who drowns in water. It actually means to be completely immersed in water. Sprinkling came from the alteration of the divine standard by the Roman Catholic Church. This is wrong, for the church does not have the responsibility to alter biblical order. Neither is baptism used as a means for a person to identify membership with a particular church.

It should be noted that water baptism in itself does not make one born again. For we believe with our hearts unto righteousness, and with our mouth confession is made unto salvation *(Rom 10:10).* Water baptism then becomes a public declaration that one is saved, and the baptized must continually walk in righteousness to stay saved. John challenged the Pharisees coming for baptism to continually bring forth fruits that proves they have genuinely repented *(Matt 3:8).* It is an act of righteousness demanded from every believer: ***"And He said to them, "Go into all the world and preach the gospel to every creature. Whoever believes and is baptized will be saved, but whoever does not believe will be condemned"" Mark 16:15-16 BSB.*** Its importance and relevance are such that even Jesus subjected Himself to it:

At that time Jesus came from Galilee to the Jordan to be baptized by John. But John tried to prevent Him, saying, "I need to be baptized by You, and do You come to me?" "Let it be so now," Jesus replied. "It is fitting for us to fulfill all righteousness in this way." Then John permitted Him. As soon as Jesus was baptized, He went up out of the water. Suddenly the heavens were opened, and He saw the Spirit of God descending like a dove and resting on Him. And a voice from heaven said, "This is My beloved Son, in whom I am well pleased!" Matt 3:13-17 BSB

God was extremely pleased with Jesus subjecting Himself to be baptized so as to fulfill all righteousness. The voice heard and the Spirit coming on Him were the evidences of His approval. This would imply refusing to be baptized is disobedience and rebellion to scripture –cannot be explained otherwise. And every rebellion to the demands of God's word is sin. Be baptized and do not forget it is by immersion.

F- The Teaching Mandate

This is very pivotal in the Great Commission. This is the pillar for discipleship of young converts. Jesus emphasized what they should be teaching – all that which He has commanded them. This matures the believer and helps him to have a glorious walk with the Lord in this temporal world. Through this teaching mandate, ignorance of divine truth is dismantled. Many have been limited because of ignorance. Teachings opens new vistas through which we get a better and bigger view to life.

A generation without teaching priests is a generation that will lose its preservation at the dawn of adversaries. Values are only reinforced and passed down to generations through teaching and living by them:

As important as this mandate is, many have taken it lightly. Jesus was very careful with regards to what and how He taught His disciples. The truth of the gospel is preserved principally from generation to generation by the teaching ministry. Bible says at some point in Israel's history as a nation, God was not with them. Consequently, they experienced troubles and oppressions from surrounding nations. This was because of the lack of teaching priests, and the lack of the consciousness of God's law *(2 Chr 15:3).*

A generation without teaching priests is a generation that will lose its preservation at the dawn of adversaries. Values are only reinforced and passed down to generations through teaching and living by them: ***"Whatever you have learned or received or heard from me, or seen in me -put it into practice. And the God of peace will be with you." Phi 4:9 NIV.*** Paul also cautioned Timothy to make sure the teachings he has learned from him, that he commits it into the hands of faithful men who will intend teach others *(2 Tim 2:2).*

G- The All-Believers Mandate

By this, we mean it was never a commission given to particular individuals, but to every member within the body of Christ. Soul-winning is one of the marks of a true disciple and follower of Jesus Christ. It is irreconcilable to be saved by the precious blood of the Lamb, and relegate soul-winning to a particular few. It would be an undeniable sign of ungratefulness to the sacrificial work of Christ for one's soul. Peter emphasized; ***"But you are a chosen race, a royal priesthood, a holy nation, God's own people, in order that you may proclaim the mighty acts of him who called you out of darkness into his marvelous light." 1 Pet 2:9 NRSV***

The only person exempted from sharing the gospel of Jesus Christ is he who has not yet been saved. For all those who have been saved are mandated by the sacrificial love of Christ for their souls to go out and testify of God's saving grace for their lives. That is what is needed to bring the light of the gospel to lost humanity, so they too can experience the saving grace of the Lord. No one is actually exempted from this, irrespective of what your pastor taught you during doctrinal classes.

Christ secret unleashed to Paul about the communion table

There is a deeper secret about the communion table that many have not understood. As a result, they have not been able to reap the full benefits that partaking in the Lord's table does for the believer. Consequently, partaking in the Lord's supper (communion table) has become a mere religious activity by many. Even those who have never surrendered their lives to Christ's lordship have become constant partakers of the Lord's table. It has now become a means of identifying with a particular denomination. This is an abuse of the Lord's table.

Fellowshipping with the saints and with the Lord on the communion table, emphasized the mandate of proclaiming the gospel: ***"For I received from the Lord what I also passed on to you: The Lord Jesus, on the night He was betrayed, took bread, and when He had given thanks, He broke it and said, "This is My***

body, which is for you; do this in remembrance of Me." In the same way, after supper He took the cup, saying, "This cup is the new covenant in My blood; do this, as often as you drink it, in remembrance of Me." For as often as you eat this bread and drink this cup, you proclaim the Lord's death until He comes." 1 Cor 11:23-26 BSB

> **It is insensitivity to the work of the cross and disobedience to the divine order to partake of the communion table and shut our mouths from witnessing for the Lord. This is the responsibility of all.**

Paul is emphasizing here that as often as we eat this bread and drink the cup, we ought to proclaim the Lord's death until He comes. This is a deep truth many have not been awakened to.

Therefore, it is insensitivity to the work of the cross and disobedience to the divine order to partake of the communion table and shut our mouths from witnessing for the Lord. This is the responsibility of all.

Those who have not been involved with evangelism because they felt it was not their calling, are mistaken. Many have not understood ***Eph 4:11(NRSV), "The gifts he gave were that some would be apostles, some prophets, some evangelists, some pastors, and teachers, to equip the saints for the work of ministry..."*** Apostles, prophets, evangelists, pastors, and teachers, are different offices within the ministry. The aim of these different offices, is to equip the saints for the work of the ministry – soul-winning and discipleship. The entirety of ministry has to do principally with saving lives, and discipling them to walk in the footsteps of Jesus Christ. What many have not known is that you do not have to occupy any of these offices to be actively involved in soul-winning and discipleship. There are lots of believers in the market place. That's supposed to be one of their primary missions fields, where they ought to focus on bringing Christ to all those in that field through diverse approaches.

A medical doctor who at his duty post (hospital) only practices medicine without the consciousness and strategies of saving the souls of the patients hasn't yet answered the call of God for being there.

These different ministry offices are designed to train and equip the believers on how to effectively win and disciple all those in their market place, for that is where the real work of the ministry is supposed to be carried out. Their jobs reveal their profession, meanwhile their relationship with the Lord reveals their ministry in the market place.

When there is a passion and consciousness to save souls, strategies would be diverse.

This would mean a medical doctor who at his duty post (hospital) only practices medicine without the consciousness and strategies of saving the souls of the patients hasn't yet answered the call of God for being there.

There is never a shortage of strategies nor resources to save souls, but an unwilling and disobedient heart! The only needed resource is an open mouth:

It is important to know that when there is a passion and consciousness to save souls, strategies would be diverse. There is no excuse not to save souls irrespective of the environment.

There is never a shortage of strategies nor resources to save souls, but an unwilling and disobedient heart! The only needed resource is an open mouth:

When God wanted to use Isaiah to take the gospel to the entire nation, all He needed was the willingness on Isaiah's part. And that is exactly what the Lord needs from us today to be used of Him to take the Goodnews to the lost: ***"Then I said: "Woe is me, for I am ruined, because I am a man of unclean lips…" Then one of the seraphim flew to me, and in his hand was a glowing coal that he had taken with tongs from the altar. And with it he touched my mouth… Then I heard the voice of the Lord saying: "Whom shall I send? Who will go for Us?" And I said: "Here am I. Send me!"" Is 6:5-8 BSB***

QUESTIONS

1. What is the Great Commission?
2. And this is life eternal, that they may know thee_______________ and Jesus Christ________?
3. Give five reasons why the Great Commission is thus considered Great?
4. What are the seven mandates stipulated within the Great Commission?
5. Not to be prepared at all times according to the "GO" Mandate is contrary to the Great Commission. True or False?
6. What do you understand as "Hit and Run?"
7. Which mandate ensures the Great Commission goes to all ethnic groups?
8. What are the four factors a missionary evangelist must be aware of to succeed in a new culture?
9. What is water baptism, and who is qualified to be baptized?
10. Not every believer is obligated to evangelize. True or False?

CHAPTER 2

THE PREPAREDNESS OF THE EVANGELIST

Principle 3: Be Ready at All Times

Evangelism is one of those aspects of the Christian faith that must be taken with lots of urgency. This is principally because it has to do with the eternal destiny of a soul, and the restoration of fellowship between the individual and the Lord Almighty. It must always be taken urgently. Nothing else is ever worth the priority than it.

This would mean that whenever the opportunity presents itself to share the gospel to an individual, every other thing can wait! We have to be alert at all times to be able to identify the opportunities that presents us the possibility of witnessing to an individual.

CREATE THE OPPORTUNITIES

We cannot wait for opportunities to witness for Christ, we rather have to create the opportunities.

Waiting for opportunities to witness for Christ is not being conscious of the Great Commission. Meeting a sinner and going without witnessing to them is doing exactly what the Priest and Levite did when they met the man laying half dead – they passed another road.

Waiting for opportunities to witness for Christ is not being conscious of the Great Commission. Meeting a sinner and going without witnessing to them is doing exactly what the Priest and Levite did when they met the man laying half dead – they passed another road.

I remember being a student in the university, every time the lecturer was not in class and I realized the students were just being idle, I stepped in and preached to the entire class. I would tell other believers that they should look out for those who will confess the Lord Jesus Christ and get their names and numbers for subsequent follow-up. But they will be too shy to do that giving me the excuse that we can't just get up and preach without first of all previously gathering in intercession and bound the strongman. My response to them always was that I bound the strongman the previous night while praying.

I wasn't ready to let go any opportunity to make the Lord known. For we have to seize the moments and create the opportunity, for that same moment with those same people may never come again.

The consciousness of soul-winning is being instant in season and out of season. Anything less is negligence and taking the shed blood of Christ for a joke.

The consciousness of soul-winning is being instant in season and out of season. Anything less is negligence and taking the shed blood of Christ for a joke.

It's important to be aware that different moments present different open doors to the hearts of specific individuals. To some people, the door may be open when they are grieving, celebrating, idling, lonely, etc. Seize every moment to share the gospel. The deceit of the devil to many believers is that they might not have been called as an evangelist, so they should stay on their lane and leave evangelism to the called. Timothy who was not an evangelist, but was told to do the work of an evangelist *(2 Tim 4:5).* We too must do same. Paul said to Agrippa, ***"I did not prove disobedient to the heavenly vision." Acts 26:19 NASB.***

Consider Philip; he responded immediately when he was told about the eunuch from Ethiopia. Whatever did occupy him at the time, became secondary. He let it go to immediately respond to the instruction of the Lord, as he began running to catch up with him *(Acts 8:26-39).* You can see his response to soul-winning was spontaneous. This is one of the characteristics of an evangelist, or an individual who has understood the importance of the Great Commission, and who has the consciousness of eternity. They are always spontaneous when it concerns souls being saved. They will not wait for a fair weather before reaching out to a lost soul. Even in their inconvenience, they give over their lives to make Christ and His sacrificial work on the cross known.

Should one wait to be instructed to evangelize?

Looking at the case of Philip, the instruction of the Lord to him was a prophetic message. This is because he did not know was any Ethiopian eunuch who had come all the way to worship in Jerusalem and was returning. The eunuch was not even in the vicinity of Philip. So, it had to be a message of revelation. His obedience to the message and the directions he was given brought him in contact with the eunuch. Other than this specific instance, evangelism is always spontaneous. That does not mean you will not listen to the Spirit of God to lead. But listening to Him, you realize that one of His ways of leading us into doing the right thing, is to cause us to have the understanding about the right thing to be done. Hence, it does leaves us with the responsibility to go ahead at once and have it done. We are admonished not to be like the horse or the mule that lacks understanding, which always needs a bit and bridle in its mouth for direction *(Psalm 32:9).*

It was understanding of our responsibility to the Great Commission that caused Paul to say, ***"Yet when I preach the gospel, I have no reason to boast, because I am obligated to preach. Woe to me if I do not preach the gospel! If my preaching is voluntary, I have a reward. But if it is [not] voluntary, I am still entrusted with a responsibility." 1 Cor 9:16-17 BSB***

He understood it was his responsibility to save souls, whether voluntarily or not. Because of this consciousness and the power of the gospel to save and transform lives, he made up his mind never to be ashamed of proclaiming it *(Rom 1:16).* Being ashamed of the gospel by failing to take on the responsibility of making Christ known, causes Christ to be ashamed of us before His Father and His holy angels *(Lk 9:26-27).* This brings us to a place of accountability and judgment before the Lord, as to why we failed to do so. Every time the gospel is being preached; a book of remembrance is written about that *(Mal 3:16).* The blood of those who died without salvation, whom we had the opportunity of witnessing to but did not, comes on our head *(Ez 3:18).*

Shutting our mouth from sharing the gospel every time we are around unbelievers is falling short of divine expectations and gross disobedience to God.

Many are not conscious of this truth, and so excuse themselves that it was written in the Old Testament. But if it was not a New Testament reality as well, Paul will not be emphasizing the fact that his life will be in problems if he preaches not the gospel. He also talked of being free from the blood of all men because he did not hesitate to preach to them the total counsel of God *(Acts 20:26).*

Therefore, shutting our mouth from sharing the gospel every time we are around unbelievers is falling short of divine expectations and gross disobedience to God.

I remember the story of two girls who were best of friends, whom I will identify as Amy and Haley. They were always together, dressing alike, and doing things together. Haley was saved and Amy weren't. Unfortunately, Haley never did anything to ensure that Amy accepts the gospel of Jesus Christ. In fact, Haley never even preached to Amy. One night, after Haley separated with Amy, she drove herself home and Amy did likewise. When Haley slept, she had a dream that Amy her best friend was talking to her angrily from hell, asking her why she never preached to her when she knew that it is only through Jesus Christ that an individual can get saved. Amy talked with vexation of spirits and said it is now she had realized that Haley never treated her as a friend, talk less as best of friends, but as an enemy. She blamed Haley for the reason she was now in hell. Haley woke up from the dream and it appeared so real. She could almost smell Sulphur and brimstone. She decided she was going to preach to her friend the next day. Early, in the morning, she called her friend on phone, but someone else picked the call. It was someone who lives in the house of her friend. When she asked to be passed to her friend, she heard sobbing on the phone. Panicking and asking why the sobbing, she was told that while she separated with her friend last night, on her way home, she had an accident and died at the spot. It was in deed a shock to Haley as she cried and felt she is responsible for her friend being in hell. She found it difficult to forgive herself.

There is no other definition of cowardice than being ashamed of what you believe.

In fact, there is no other definition of cowardice than being ashamed of what you believe. To be ashamed of what you believe, is a criminal offence punishable by the court of heaven.

Praying that God will speak to us whether or not to evangelize a particular individual, and when to, is a false perspective and unscriptural.

Generally speaking, this would mean that praying that God will speak to us whether or not to evangelize a particular individual, and when to, is a false perspective and unscriptural. For now, is the day of salvation *(2 Cor 6:2)*, and we have to be ready at all times to give an answer of our hope in Christ *(1 Pe 3:15)*.

Principle 4: Identify and Seize the Door of Opportunity

Any time an individual seems interested in you, it becomes an opportunity to seize and share the gospel of the Lord Jesus Christ with him or her. Such moments must not be left to go by. There are indeed pockets of doors of opportunities that presents themselves to us daily. All we need to do is be spontaneous to identify those doors and act immediately. This is because a particular door being opened, might be the only door that could cause the individual in question to have an open heart to the gospel. A moment later, once the door is closed, you bring the same gospel to the individual, he or she may not even want to hear it. That is why the scriptures admonishes us with regards to preaching the gospel, to be spontaneous in season and out of season *(2 Tim 4:2).* This is also the reason why the word of God is quick (spontaneous) and powerful (not limited by change of seasons), as mentioned in *(Heb 4:12).*

When people go through certain seasons in their lives, certain doors open with those particular seasons.

It is important to know that when people go through certain seasons in their lives, certain doors open with those particular seasons. That is the reason why God will allow people to experience certain seasonal challenges and changes.

To postpone witnessing to a person when opportunities arise is gross betrayal to divine plans and wisdom to save a soul.

To postpone witnessing to a person when opportunities arise is gross betrayal to divine plans and wisdom to save a soul.

Remember Peter took advantage of the time the multitude gathered mocking the disciples that they were drunk. All this because the Holy Spirit came on them, and they began speaking in tongues about the wonders of God in the various native languages of the people. Languages that they had never learned. Though they mocked them, yet they were bewildered since the disciples were accurately speaking in languages they never learned. So, they were really amazed about the miracle. Peter saw it as a great door of opportunity to explain to them what was going on.

Peter began from the point of their bewilderment to answer the worries in their minds and hearts. He then explains to them the truth of Jesus Christ. He didn't spend time to debate their theological viewpoint, but provided the answer to their questions and drove the good news of Christ to their hearts. The result was that they were convicted of their sins and repented *(Acts 2:11-41).* The same day three thousand more believers were added to the church.

Imagine what could have happened if Peter had not taken advantage of the opened door, and rather postponed his preaching to them for the next day? The following would have been the possible outcome:

i. He would not have met all of them as they would have all retired to where they had come from to partake of the regular feast of Pentecost that was being held annually.

ii. It would have been difficult to assemble the people together. And any attempt of assembling the people could have incurred costs, as they may need to print fliers, radio announcements, etc.

Every opportunity to win souls is strategic as it facilitates the soul-winning process without unnecessary expenditures.

Seizing every opportunity to win souls is strategic as it facilitates the soul-winning process without unnecessary expenditures. Therefore, lack of resources to do the work of the Lord cannot be blamed on God. It could be an indication that the minister is not sensitive to the leading of the Spirit and the opportunities that surrounds him. For God will never give a vision and keep from it the provision. Hence, rather than spend precious moments simply praying for provision, pray first that the Lord help you to become sensitive to the opportunities that come your way to serve Him. For there is a time of life that comes to everyone during which every resource needed for the purposes of God are readily available. What gives you access to those resources is your level of spontaneous obedience to the Lord's service.

iii. It would have been difficult to get all the people focus on one thing, as many of them would have had other activities distracting them.

iv. (iv)-It would have been difficult to engage them again into a discussion.

v. The people's hearts would have become more hardened as they would have slept on the preconceived idea that they were drunk, and the enemy would have preyed on their minds about those thoughts and convinced them more that the believers were drunkards. It would close their hearts more towards the gospel, because what sense can a drunkard make?

vi. The encouragement of one another towards their conversion would not have been there since many of them would not have been present again. This is because when people live more or less in a community of friends, customs, cultures, hobbies, trades, the conversion of one can positively influence the conversion of the others.

vii. The encouragement of the apostles one to another would not have been there, because some of the apostles could have dispersed.

Peter took advantage of the opportunity, and the rest eleven stood with him. God has always designed to work in a team, and Himself is a team. The Scriptures are clear on this when it says about God creating man, ***"Let US create man in OUR image and in OUR likeness..." (Gen 1:26),*** and of Christ to His disciples, ***"We all must work the works of Him who sent Me..." (Jn 9:4).***

(viii)-The conviction factor might not have been much again because the peoples' receptivity would have also dwindled. The conviction factor has always been ascribed both on the work of the Holy Spirit on the heart of the individual, and the current moment.

A true soul-winner places conversion priority over disputable matters of doctrines, as he contends for the souls of men at all cost.

Paul emphasized that now is the day of salvation *(2 Cor 6:2).* The author of Hebrews reiterated that if you hear His voice today, do not harden your hearts *(Heb 3:15).* It is thus vital for the minister to be super sensitive to when the Holy Spirit has prepared the hearts of the people for conversion, so as to take advantage of the moment and lead them to the Lord. Just as

God in the creation account knew exactly when to command the various elements of creation into being. Most believers fail to identify the conversion points of individuals as they bring the Goodnews to them. They preach to an individual into and out of conviction. They seem more excited delivering the sermon than saving their souls.

A true soul-winner places conversion priority over disputable matters of doctrines, as he contends for the souls of men at all cost.

Postponing taking advantage of doors of opportunities to save souls is insensitivity to the Holy Spirit, disobedience, and lack of compassion for the souls of men. It cannot be explained otherwise.

The goal of the evangelist is not to finish preaching his sermon, but knowing exactly when to offer the alter call. If Peter did not take advantage of the door of opportunity as seen in *(Acts 2:8-11)*, and the right time to present the alter call (when the people were convicted in their hearts) as seen in *(Acts 2:37)*, they would have lost these three thousand souls. This could be indicative of the fact that most churches might have not grown because the leaders didn't understand when the doors of ministry (doors of opportunities) were opened to them so they could take advantage of. Before they realize it, the doors got closed. While some might have identified the doors, but administrative bottlenecks became the reason while the doors got closed. It is important to note that opportunities only last for a particular period of time. They hardly go for a longer period of time.

Postponing taking advantage of doors of opportunities to save souls is insensitivity to the Holy Spirit, disobedience, and lack of compassion for the souls of men. It cannot be explained otherwise.

Know that soul winning must be taken spontaneously with urgency. It is like ministering to people like the man who was left half-dead by thieves who attacked him on the road from Jerusalem to Jericho *(Lk 10:25-37).* This is because the passing of every minute will lead to his death (eternal loss of his soul). Paul admonished us with regards to engaging for the salvation of souls, not to be foolish in wasting time, but to redeem the times for the days are evil *(Eph 5:16-17).*

Crazy is the politest definition of bureaucracy when it comes to engaging for the salvation of souls.

Crazy is the politest definition of bureaucracy when it comes to engaging for the salvation of souls. God warned me years ago never to halt my outreach programs because of lack of resources, but that He will meet me in the field and provide. And He has always been faithful. I remembered flying to Tanzania without enough money for my visa on arrival. After landing, I stood on the cue to obtain my visa confused of where I will get money for the visa fee. Then the man who was standing behind me on the cue said he will pay my fee. He was someone I had preached to while in the flight. God showed up!

"The Time of Life"

This is the time and season where it's much easier for anyone to succeed in whatever they have been called for. Resources are readily available if the individual is determined and more persuasive. It is a time that God has strategically positioned certain things the individual needs for the assignment. All he needs to do to access all that is available for him in that moment, is to be sensitive to the leadings of the Spirit, and arise and seize the available opportunities.

"To everything there is a season, and a time for every purpose under heaven...He has made everything beautiful in its time..." Ecc 3:1,11 BSB. Due to this, the Scriptures admonishes us to be alert at all times *(1 Pet 1:13).*

With regards to the concept of "The Time of Life," Abraham had received a word of prophecy from the Lord that he will become a father of nations, yet twenty-four years went by without the prophecy being fulfilled. One day, he was visited by three men, not knowing that the answer to that long-awaited prophecy laid in the manner in which he will receive them.

Being a genuine God-lover and one whom the Lord had worked on his heart, he did not only receive them, but he honored them by the manner in which he received them - demanding that the fattest calf be killed for them. He did not ask for the leftover food to be served for them, but he engaged his whole household to prioritize attending to their needs. This is what the Bible says that he who receives a prophet as a prophet, receives a prophet's reward (Matt 10:41). This is specific to the honor in which he receives the prophet, else, it would not have added the conditional clause, ***"as a prophet.*** "This should be an eye-opener, because often, even when we receive people and show some hospitality, we do it dishonorably - as though someone was forcing us. David understood this principle, and that is why he treated the house of God with honor – ***"I was glad when they said let us go into the house of the Lord" (Psalm 122:1).*** Even Jesus honored the house of the Lord and the manner in which He handled the scroll *(Lk 4:18-19).*

The manner in which Abraham received these three men, triggered his miracle. They told him with specificity that by this same time next year, he will have a child, according to the time of life. The question is why specifically by this same time next year? It's so that he can remember that the miracle was activated based on the manner in which he received them (without even knowing they were angels). This would mean it was going to be a memorable event for him. So, every time Isaac's birthday is coming, Abraham would remember that his birth was only possible because of the love and honor He accorded to these men. This is therefore indicative that many have received prophecies from God which never got manifested in the physical, simply because of dishonor to the things of God, dishonor to humanity, and having no regards for people. The Scriptures reiterate that if your brother comes to you hungry and all you say is go well fed without offering him help (when you are able to), then you have not the love of God *(1 Jn 3:17).* Jesus told the woman of Samaria that if she only knew the gift of God and who He was that asked for a drink, she would have asked of Him and He would have given her life-giving water *(Jn 4:10).* This would mean every opportunity to minister to the needs of men, especially spiritual needs, is an opportunity to minister to God. Therefore, it becomes the same opportunity for you to receive that which your soul genuinely yearns for from the Lord.

Protocol Team

Considering the manner in which Abraham received these three men, is quite inspiring. It is very important for every ministry to develop a protocol team. This is a team that receives visiting servants of God, as well as guests. They should be well trained on how to honor guests in ways that makes them feel welcome and celebrated. This is far from human worship. It must be done in a spirit of holiness, stewardship, and prayer. It has a way of opening the spirit of the minister and giving him the liberty to tap into the bowels of anointing in him to function. Honoring the minister has a way of helping the individual to benefit from the anointing upon the life of the minister. The Jewish people understood the importance of honoring guests to the extent of washing the feet of those who visited them (Jn 13:1-17). They will not just give the individuals water to wash their feet by themselves, but they will wash it for them. Jesus told the disciples that any house that they go to that refuses to receive them, they should shake the dusts off their feet as a testimony against the inhabitants of the house (Matt 10:14). Shaking the dust off their feet proves they were not received, else, their feet would have been washed.

Though it is honorable to receive ministers, yet no minister should set his heart on that. Neither should he have an attitude when he is not received in an honorable way. Else, that will be pride on his part. It should be done voluntarily by the one receiving him. The one receiving him also determines the parameters and extent to which he wants to do that. One time I visited a country for the launching of ***Operation Last Hour Rescue Vision*** (which is a vision to get chaplains into hospitals and nursing homes so that no person in those facilities dies without experiencing salvation). The pastors did receive me and allocated a protocol team that went with me everywhere, day and night. I realize it was very important as it helps in self-accountability, and how I did relate and welcome those who wanted to meet with me, especially females. It helps to protect the minister emotionally because he becomes double conscious and anyone visiting him is double conscious as well. Though every minister must set his heart on doing right and running away from every appearance of evil.

It also prepares the spirits of the people to receive the ministration from the minister. Because the way in which they see the minister being honored, it helps portrays how valuable the gift of God in him is. Therefore, it increases their expectations and opens their spirits to easily receive from the minister. When Jesus went to His hometown, He was not received with honor. Consequently, no matter how much He tried to do many mighty works, He could not because of the unbelief of the people *(Matt 13:58).*

The only challenge with this kind of reception is that the masses may think it is human worship and may blame it on the individual being received. But every ministry must well educate the people as to why it is necessary. There was a time that I did not think that manner of honorable reception was important. But by maturing in my understanding of scriptures with regards to ministry, I saw the relevance of it. Though certain parameters must also be observed by the ministry presenting such reception to its guests so as not to place more value on the individual than on God. For many ministers have abused it and have given conditions on how they should be received, the kind of cars to pick them up from the airport, etc. As earlier indicated, it's the team that receives the minister that decides on how to do it, and not the minister himself. Be on your guard for anyone who tells you how he would want to be received!

Some ministers have found themselves in situations that they begin to emphasized how they want to be received because they feel they have had past experiences wherein they felt taken for granted. With that still, it doesn't justify them emphasizing how they want to be received. Ministry cannot be done effectively if we do not put on humility from the inward man and are ready to lay down our lives for Christ.

Valuing The Minister's Role

The minister being received also should realize that honor is earned not solicited for. People honor others automatically and spontaneously based on the difference the individuals being honored have created. People are being honored for what they have done, their successes, their endurance and tenacity. Mandela was honored for his tenacity and endurance of pursuing the freedom of his people from apartheid even to the point he willingly accepted being in prison and the willingness to die for the liberation of South Africans. Paul told Timothy to show forth himself as an example to the believers (1 Tim 4:11). Only then will his profiting become evident to all. So, rather than craving for honor, crave to fulfil purpose and be an example, then honor will follow.

On the contrary, honor is easily lost if the minister being honored becomes indisciplined with his life and principles. Paul cautioned Timothy to watch his manner of life and doctrine closely. It is quite costly and demanding for any individual to rise to a position of honor. But in a matter of minutes, compromise on his values and principles could bring him down and make him to be resented by the people. That is the reason why certain open doors gets closed to the same person.

Transparency and genuineness from the heart are factors that every great leader must possess, if he will secure the continuous trust and loyalty of the people.

Therefore, transparency and genuineness from the heart are factors that every great leader must possess, if he will secure the continuous trust and loyalty of the people.

Principle 5: Be Prompt and Instantaneous to Obey

The Great Commission necessitates a prompt and quick response. It is this level of commitment and seriousness that portrays that the believer has fully understood its greatness. Many have treated the issue of soul-winning as though they will always have the time for it. It is true there always will be souls to be saved whenever we chose to reach them. But that is no excuse if we will not be prompt now to reach out to all those we can. This is because though there always will be souls to saved whatever the day and time we chose to reach out, many others who could have had the opportunity to be preached to, might have died.

The true spirit of a soul-winner is never at rest every time someone who could have been saved, didn't get saved, or an opportunity to witness to someone goes by. Therefore, being prompt and instantaneous is of the essence.

The true spirit of a soul-winner is never at rest every time someone who could have been saved, didn't get saved, or an opportunity to witness to someone goes by.

QUESTIONS

1. What are the two reasons why evangelism must be taken urgently?
2. Waiting for opportunities to witness for Christ instead of creating them is being conscious of the Great Commission. True or False?
3. ***"Yet when I preach the gospel, I have no reason to boast, because I am obligated to preach."*** Where is it found in the scriptures?
4. Different seasons in people's lives present certain open doors to each them. True or False?
5. Five possible things happening if Peter had postponed his preaching in Acts 2:11-41?
6. In your own words, what is ***"The time of Life"*** for the evangelizing of a particular soul?
7. What are the two most important factors a leader needs to secure trust and loyalty from his people?
8. The goal of the evangelist is to finish preaching his sermon first before issuing the alter call. True or False?
9. Honoring a minister helps you benefit from the anointing upon him. True or False?
10. What is the politest definition of bureaucracy in engaging to save a soul?

CHAPTER 3

PRIORITY OF THE SOUL-WINNER

Principle 6: Avoid Interruptions on Path to Soul-Winning

In every field, focus is important if realizing the objectives will be attainable. Philip was sent by the Lord to reach out to the eunuch who was already on his journey back to his country. What a demanding mission. The question is why will God commission a man for such a mission after a eunuch who is in his chariot back home. More to that, Philip does not have a chariot or any means of transportation. If Philip would not be able to meetup with the eunuch simply because he was on foot, logically it would be well understood. But when the Lord commissioned him, he realizes that much is demanded from him. He had to do everything possible to meetup with the eunuch. With such a timely assignment, he realized that what he would not be allowed to attend to will be every form of distractions.

Truth be told, every time there is an assignment commissioned to a person, sudden distractions of all sorts begin to show forth - especially when it has to do with soul-winning and advancing the kingdom of God. This is so because the enemy does not want believers to be given to soul-winning. The evangelist or soul-winner must be fully aware of this. Many had set out for soul-winning only to find themselves being occupied with seemingly important Christian activities. The enemy is quite smart. He would get the believer occupied with other Christian activities other than soul-winning. Jesus rebuked Martha that she was busy with cooking and many other things which were not as important as the one thing Mary had chosen, which was sitting at His feet and listening to the word of God *(Lk 10:38-42).* Jesus Himself at one time was busy teaching the word of God to the people when His family showed up demanding to see Him. He refused to attend to them as He emphasized that His family were those who were seated listening to His teachings *(Matt 12:46-50).* The question is why could they not wait for Him to be done teaching the people before desiring to talk with Him?

Scriptures makes it clear that anyone who puts his hand on the plow and looks backward, is not fit for the kingdom. That has to do with distraction. We will never be effective in ministry and approved for higher heights of exploits if we still tolerate distractions in our lives. When Elisha the prophet sent Gehazi to go raise the dead son of a certain woman, he commanded him not to greet anyone on the way *(2 Ki 4:29).*

Our determination to put away all forms of distractions is an expression of how much we value the salvation of men, the ministry, and the calling of God upon our lives. Paul thanked the Lord for considering him faithful and calling him into His service to make Christ known to the lost (1 Tim 1:12). No doubt he was focused and avoided distractions.

Demands Of the Soul-Winning Ministry

Due to the demands of the ministry, one must avoid distractions of all sorts. Irrespective of your specific calling, there is a great demand upon your life for soul-winning. Everything you do for the ministry must be aimed principally at getting more souls for the kingdom.

The gospel is the power of salvation unto all men. The greatest love we can demonstrate to an individual is to present them with this glorious gospel for the salvation of their souls.

Meeting a person and discussing everything else without ensuring if he has a relationship with the Lord Jesus is a total waste of his time – even if he is not aware of, for eternity will reveal that to him!

Meeting a person and discussing everything else without ensuring if he has a relationship with the Lord Jesus is a total waste of his time – even if he is not aware of, for eternity will reveal that to him! God is delighted in seeing us witnessing to lives daily at all times, to the extent that a book of remembrance is being opened and noted *(Mal 3:16).* In fact, there is great joy in heaven over a soul that repents. Winning souls daily is actually making God's day! No doubt He says there is great joy in heaven over one sinner who repents *(Lk 15:7).* Not to be involved in winning souls for the kingdom is the Great Disobedience.

I remembered years ago on a bus, I was so tired and in a fast. I had been evangelizing the whole day and was going back home. I asked the Lord if He still wanted me to share the gospel in the taxi. After I asked that question, a great silence followed after in my spirit. I could sense literally the quietness of God, when suddenly a voice spoke to me saying, ***"What kind of question is that? Are you asking me whether you should win souls?"*** Immediately I felt ashamed as I could feel the emotions of God expressed through the silence. I had to then preach again in the taxi, and my spirit was revived afterward. I felt an amazing strength that came to me. God is so concerned about soul-winning, and so must we. Jesus summarized

His total purpose for coming into the world: ***"The Son of man is come to seek and to save that which is lost." Luke 19:10.***

It is Worth the Commitment

One day when Jesus was passing through the city of Jericho, one tax collector by the name of Zacchaeus wanted to see Him, but the people would not want that to happen. So, ran ahead and climbed up a sycamore tree to see Him. Though Zacchaeus was a sinner and rejected by the people, Jesus chose not to bypass him. He decided to cancel every other program He had for the day so as to be able to stay in the house of Zacchaeus. He realized that he needed salvation, and if it must entail Him spending the night in his house, then so be it.

Beloved, when it comes to soul-winning, your total commitment and engagement is needed. You can never afford to treat it like the last thing on your list. In my youthful days, I decided that the only proof that I went somewhere would be to present the Lord with souls won from there. You can't afford to meet unbelievers and not bring them the gospel. For if they are aware of the importance of eternal salvation, they will do everything to get you preach to them. Therefore, evangelizing is not something to joke with. If you are reading this book, the least God will expect from you is to respond to this great call to soul-winning. I remember Elie Wiesel once said; ***"Every time I am without a chisel, I feel guilty."*** He was a stone cutter, and was very ready to cut stones any day and any time. That's the same way we ought to be conscious about our primary assignment; soul-winning.

QUESTIONS

1. Entertain interruptions when going out to win souls. True or False?
2. Other Christian activities equates soul-sinning. True or False?
3. Under what circumstances did Jesus rebuke Martha?
4. What is the greatest love we can portray to an individual?
5. What Scripture proofs Jesus's mandate was to win souls for the Lord?
6. Soul-winning can be the last thing on your list of your daily schedule. True or False?
7. What did Elie Wiesel say about not having a chisel with him?
8. Who did Jesus say is His family?
9. What would you consider a distraction on path to soul-winning?
10. If you have a different calling, then do not bother to evangelize. True or False?

CHAPTER 4

THE THREE-FOLD PERSON

It is important to note that every individual you will ever meet, is a three-fold individual. By three-fold, I mean he or she has *a Past Life, a Present Life*, and the anticipation of *a Future Life*. None of these should be ignored as though it does not matter. The individual's response to the gospel will be based on these three active phases of his life. Therefore, the evangelist needs to be very skilled on handling these three important phases in the person's life if witnessing to him or her will be effective.

These three phases could be very well handled in details at the stage of discipleship after, as it may demand more time. Discipling the individual after he or she has made a prior commitment for the Lord is of great necessity. Notwithstanding, the evangelist must be very sensitive in witnessing to the individual as the Holy Spirit could give him insights into things and make him share on particular subjects that he can relate with; either with their past, present, or an anticipated future. This will cause them to be more open and receptive to the gospel, as opposed to them not being able to relate with whatsoever the evangelist is trying to communicate.

A biblical example of a three-fold ministration

The story of the woman who was brought to Jesus to have been caught in the very act of adultery. The Pharisees had stones in their hands in readiness to stone her, but they wanted to hear what Jesus had to say about their intention of stoning her. She was at the verge of losing her life to her accusers. Looking at her situation, much can be identified, which was quite traumatic for her. It was not only that she was to be stoned, but she was also being discriminated against; the man she was caught with was spared by the Pharisees. She felt the reality of prejudice and gender discrimination from those she least expected.

When she was finally brought to Jesus, they explained to Him what happened. But Jesus discerned the whole situation and the fact that her accusers were biased against her as they let go of the man. Jesus said that if anyone is without sin, he should be the first to throw the stone at her. They all left one after the other. Jesus, based on what He said that made her accusers left, He was the only one qualified to stone her. But He did not stone her. Instead, He addressed the 3-fold dimension of her life in the following ways:

(i)- HER PAST – "NEITHER DO I CONDEMN YOU!"

Jesus knew she was already conscious of the fact that she committed a sin. So, Jesus did not keep on hitting on the same past over and over. He knew she was already psychologically troubled because of the discrimination the men (the Pharisees) showed her. He was very careful to deal with her in a way that did not project Him as one of her biased accusers. Jesus approached her past with grace, for he ministered grace to his hearers *(Eph 4:29).* For it is the love of God that brings a man to repentance *(Rom 2:4).*

Imagine Jesus the preacher of righteousness and a sinless individual, tells her He does not condemn her. What a word of grace and love. That actually shocked her and made her see the difference and uniqueness of Jesus - His love, compassion, mercy. It gave her hope again and made her appreciate the love of God.

(ii)- HER PRESENT – "GO!"

She had been kidnapped by the Pharisees, and was about to be stoned. In dealing with her present, Jesus offered her freedom - Go! That relieved her of all the tensions and the fear of being stoned. He offered her freedom. Paul told the Galatian church that it was for freedom that Christ made them free *(5:1).* It's like some load and burden fell off her shoulders. I can picture tears of surprise, joy, and freedom going down her cheeks as she blessed the Lord for giving her the chance to live again and to make things right.

Dear evangelist, people are already burdened with lots of loads, the frustrations of besetting sins, that they really do not want someone that comes to add to that burden. It is not to say you will compromise the word, but that you will point them to the cross, which offers solution and deliverance from sins. Such preaching is from a place of genuine love and not condemnation. This makes them to realize that the way out is through salvation in Christ Jesus.

(iii)- HER FUTURE – "SIN NO MORE!"

Most people who have been entangled in uncertain sins or habits, and have gotten to a place where they feel their lives cannot be better again. They feel captured beyond their ability to free themselves. That is the case of an addiction. Most of such people just want to know if their lives can become better, if they can actually experience genuine deliverance and be happy again. By telling her; ***"Sin no more,"*** gives her lots of hope and some psychological relieve. She feels empowered internally as she sees the possibility of a new life. She realizes her future is better than her past. Just as the scriptures declares that we may arise and shine for our light has come and the glory of the Lord has arisen over us

(Isaiah 60:1). For the first time a new air of freedom and possibilities surrounds her. She begins for the first-time detesting sin as she sees sin to be extremely sinful and destructive. She could not even imagine how she got into the promiscuous lifestyle. She did not only go with the decision not to sin again, but she goes testifying how Jesus saved her. Thereby becoming an evangelist.

Dearly beloved, if we will approach people with this three-fold approach in perspective as we bring the gospel of Jesus to them, then we will produce results that will be phenomenal - as they will eventually become great vessels through which God will extend His love to many others.

Principle 7: Understand Personality Differences

Peoples' personalities influence their approach to the gospel.

It should be noted that peoples' personalities influence their approach to the gospel. Even their experiences in life play a significant role. It may actually determine whether they will accept the message of the gospel or reject it. The rejection of many may be a reflection of deeply rooted pain. This pain could be as the result of hurtful experiences. And the feeling of if God really exist, then that is when they needed Him the most, if He was ever interested in them. So, their rejection of the gospel becomes a form of accusation to God for abandoning them, especially those who had been treated poorly by Christians, pastors, and believers. Their negative experiences with those who seem to profess Christianity may be the reason why they do not want to open up to the preaching of the gospel. That is why the preacher must not be hot tempered, else, he will not know how to properly manage certain situations. And he might end up getting into a quarrel or fight with them. Rather, he must be gentle, apt to teach, with a great deal of patience. All in hope that God will grant his hearers a heart of repentance due to the knowledge of the truth *(2 Tim 2:25).*

Principle 8: Peoples' Mindsets Are Preprogrammed by Their Cultures

Culture influences the way people will respond both to the gospel presented, and the preacher presenting it. People's mindsets are not only influenced by their cultures and customs, but also by their personal experiences. Due to the experiences and challenges, they have been through, it does have a strong baring on their lives with regards to the gospel. They could either be closed-up and unreceptive, or vice versa.

Many cultures already have their worldview concerning divinity and the object of their worship. Consequently, their response to the gospel is greatly affected positively or negatively by their worldview. Some cultures, though they might have a different worldview, yet are not hostile to the Christian's worldview. Their receptiveness to the Christian's worldview may attract more missionaries. Such cultures become more open to the Christian message. Many will get saved, and may even become involved in evangelizing their indigenous communities. This will result to eventual cultural shifts in certain anti-biblical aspects of their cultures. Just as what happened in the city of Ephesus in the time of Paul – so mightily grew the word of God and prevailed *(Acts 19:20).*

Wisdom on the Part of the Evangelist

In certain cases, if the culture already has its own particular worldview, they may primarily oppose the preaching of the gospel. They may rally against the missionary evangelist to either chase him away or kill him. This is one of the challenges some missionaries face when they find themselves in hostile cultures. If the missionary will succeed in his evangelistic mission to that area, he needs to fully understand the culture and the language of the people. Understanding the language will help in effectively communicating the gospel, while understanding the culture will help him understand the nature of the people, their perspectives, how they relate to a missionary, and what their possible disposition will be to the Christian message. All these will give him insight and inspirations on how to strategize to communicate properly the message to the natives in a way that will lessen hostility and opposition to the gospel.

Many have suffered unnecessary persecutions because they fail to understand these principles.

Realize that evangelism in itself is an art and science. It requires skillfulness, design, observation, and creativity on the part of the preacher for his audience to be motivated. He needs to know exactly how to bring the gospel to the heart of the individual. Notice that approaching someone is already stepping into the person's comfort zone. That in itself could be challenging. Although many people may not find a problem with

Evangelism in itself is an art and science. It requires skillfulness, design, observation, and creativity on the part of the preacher for his audience to be motivated.

someone approaching them, the evangelist needs to be very skillful on how to do that as well as what to say and how to engage the individual into a discussion. This will determine whether he will be listened to, and whether the gospel he preaches would be accepted.

How to Approach People

> **To be granted audience by an individual whom you approach with the gospel, is not a right but a privilege.**

It is important for every believer to understand that to be granted audience by an individual whom you approach with the gospel, is not a right but a privilege. This needs to be at the back of the mind of the evangelist as he approaches people. In as much as we have the right as demanded by the Scriptures to witness for Christ, it's a privileged when granted audience. Therefore, he will have to be very much friendly and respectful in his approach. The following tips are important:

(i)-Greetings

The very first thing a believer does in taking the gospel message to someone is to greet them. That's a basic ethical responsibility towards anyone you are approaching in the society, whether for the gospel or something else. It presents you as responsible, mature, and respectful.

(ii)-Introduce yourself

Most people find it difficult relating and being open to a stranger. Therefore, to both capture and secure their attention, give a brief meaningful introduction about yourself (name, what you do, where you from, and probably the church where you fellowship if necessary). People want to feel like they know something relevant about you. This brief introduction will give them a certain level of calmness and trust psychologically as they give you, their attention. It is rude approaching someone with the gospel without greeting them or without a brief introduction of yourself. If you fail to greet or introduce yourself, some will call your attention to that and may end up not listening to you. It could be humiliating for someone presenting the gospel to be rebuked for not being polite.

(iii)-Seek their consent

Most people want to feel they own the right to decide whether you should talk to them or not. They feel uncomfortable if you just jump in and start talking. So, it is necessary that you seek their opinion to talk to them about the gospel of Jesus Christ, after you must have greeted and introduced yourself. In most of the cases, they will give you the go-ahead if they are available. If they are busy, they may let you know and may either give you few minutes of their time, or may let you know they will be willing to hear you next time. At least, they will be polite in their response to you, whatever that response may be.

If their response is negative, do not try to quarrel with them on that. The least thing a soul-winner should do is to quarrel. Once you realize it is a privilege to be granted audience, then there will never be any reason for anger or quarrel because your request was turned down. Paul the apostle cautioned Timothy on this: ***"As a servant of the Lord, you must not argue. You must be kind to everyone. You must be a good teacher, and you must be patient." 2 Tim 2:24 ERV.*** If you can plead with them to listen to you for just a minute, then do. But if not, respectfully accept their decision. Never get to the point where you put on an attitude against them simply because they did not want to listen. Talk less of threatening them with harsh words or with judgmental proclamations. That will be totally wrong and may even cause the individual never to want to listen to the gospel again, even if it was a different preacher.

(iv)-Appreciate them

Irrespective of whether they permit you to share the gospel with them or not, appreciate them. Every human wants to be appreciated. If they give you their consent, appreciating them for that presents you as a well-cultured and respectful person. It influences them positively psychologically as they feel more peaceful in your presence with undivided attention. It presents you also as friendly, as some may even want to become friends with you.

Getting someone's full attention in order to share the gospel with them is really an art and a science.

In fact, getting someone's full attention in order to share the gospel with them is really an art and a science. Every believer must be trained to do that, if the gospel message is to get a hearing.

(v)-Present the Gospel

After going through the above steps present to them the gospel. If you have any reading materials(tracts), this could be the right time to hand it to them as you talk with them. Make it brief, appealing, and exciting. Present the message in a way that engages them - asking them questions, as well giving them the room to ask questions. Engage them into the dialogue, but do not allow them dominate the discussion. Else, they may drive it towards very sensitive religious topics that may just generate arguments and disagreement thereby defeating the whole purpose of evangelizing them.

As you proceed, make sure you share with them in a way that at the end, you can provide the invitation to them to make a commitment for Christ. As much as possible, encourage them to take the decision for the Lord as they listen to you. Help them to make the commitment while you are still with them. Do not just share and allow them to depart without making the commitment (as many believers are in the habit of doing), when it is possible for them to do so. Else, the enemy can easily show up and prevent them from making the commitment while they are by themselves. As he presents them with opposing thoughts contrary to what you shared with them. And since they have not yet been grounded in the word of God, they may not have the right answers to those thoughts. So, their conviction on what was preached becomes diluted, and they no longer see the need to be saved. This was exactly what Satan did to Eve – Satan corrupted her mind with regards to God's instruction for them not to eat of the tree of the knowledge of good and evil. She then began seeing its fruits as good for food *(Gen 3:1-6).*

(vi)-Pray and ask God's blessings for them

As they are willing to make the commitment for the Lord, pray with them to help them make the commitment. Give them the affirmation from scripture that with their hearts they believe unto righteousness and with their mouth, confession is made unto salvation (Rom 10:10). They need to understand that even if their sins were as scarlet, they shall be as white as snow (Isa 1:18). You have to assure them scripturally that they are now the children of God (1 Jn 3:1).

Giving them this assurance of their new found relationship in Christ is very pivotal to their Christian journey. It helps to continually reaffirm their rebirth irrespective of the deceitful thoughts from the enemy that may come to sway them. Pray also for God's blessings upon their lives, health, business, and family. It has a way of cementing everything and making them wanting to keep touch with you. Exchanging contacts with them at this point is of great importance so as to continually help them in their faith in the Lord.

Power Evangelism

Cultures that are basically not very receptive to the gospel, this will be a very good way to go. It is worth realizing that a hundred percent of people if made to know that a certain manifestation of power through miracles, healings, signs and wonders is genuinely from God, they will get excited about it. This has always been true in the Bible days as Jesus and the apostles went about doing good, healing all those who were sick. This resulted to countless salvations.

The importance of power evangelism is not only a phenomenon in the New Testament, but also of the Old Testament: ***"The LORD said unto my Lord, Sit thou at my right hand, until I make thine enemies thy footstool. The LORD shall send the rod of thy strength out of Zion: rule thou in the midst of thine enemies. Thy people shall be willing in the day of thy power…" Psalms 110:1-3 KJV.***

Jesus even promised the disciples that as they go about evangelizing, He will accompany them performing signs and wonders *(Mt 28:18-20, Mk 16:15-20).* This is a very strong weapon to bring a people who pledge allegiance to different gods into pledging allegiance to the Lord Almighty, as they realize He is the One True God. Though some people may still resist the gospel even when they see the working of miracles, yet, a greater number of people will willingly submit to the gospel when they see that. The evangelist must trust God to operate in such dimensions of power if his mission work will be successful, especially in a very religious or pagan culture.

Principle 9: Most People You Meet Have Something to Do with Religion

The reason we go to them with the preaching of the gospel is because they have the ability to believe. Even atheists do believe, just that they believe in the inexistence of God and the agnostics believe in the existence of God, but that the knowledge of Him cannot be known. So, it shouldn't surprise us if the people we do approach with the gospel do believe in the wrong things. That is why the Lord instructs us to go share with them the gospel of Jesus Christ for a change of their object of believe (if any). Paul found himself in Athens a city that was given to the worship of several objects. He approached the people of Athens and said: ***"For as I passed by, and beheld your devotions, I found an altar with this inscription, TO THE UNKNOWN GOD. Whom therefore you ignorantly worship, him declare I unto you." Acts 17:23 KJV***

It is thus evident here that different people and cultures have different objects of worship. So, the evangelist must not become offended when an individual he approached with the gospel says he does not believe nor care for what the evangelists is preaching, because he has his own beliefs. Instead, he should know how to approach him. That is why it will be of great importance for every soul-winner to study about other religious beliefs such as Islam, Buddhism, Hinduism, etc. This will help him understand the background of the person's beliefs. In that case, he will be well knowledgeable on how to present the gospel, as well as how to respond to certain questions asked.

QUESTIONS

1. What is the meaning of a three-fold person?
2. Ignoring a person's three-fold life has no effect on his response to the gospel. True or False?
3. How did Jesus minister to the three-fold life aspects of the woman caught in adultery?
4. How can a person's personality influence his response to the gospel?
5. What are some of the challenges of hostile cultures to the evangelist?
6. It is a right and not a privilege to be granted audience by a person you want to evangelize. True or False?
7. What are the six steps on how to approach someone with the gospel?
8. What New Testament Scripture portrays the importance of the power of God in evangelizing?
9. What is the believe of atheists?
10. What do you know about the city of Athens?

CHAPTER 5

RELATING WITH DIFFERENT PERSONALITIES

Principle 10: How You Relate with the Individual Determines the Outcome.

Peoples respond to you due to their portfolio, credentials, education, and social class. Hence, be careful how you approach them, and how you manage the moment while in their presence. They analyze you as you talk based on their portfolio. That is why most preachers cannot effectively minister to certain people of certain classes, even some of those they seem to have won. The person is there or offers audience because he needs healing, or a favor from God, or because he has had some personal encounters with the Lord. Therefore, to be on the safe side as you approach people, treat them with lots of love and respect, irrespective of their social strata. This is very pivotal if our communication with them is to yield any fruit.

Delicate People

Some people are very sensitive to how they are approached by others. This might be due to their level of education, experiences, cultural inclinations, and past experiences with church folks. Their attitudes can be either inviting or repulsive depending on the approach they are given.

A typical example is the woman of Samaria that Jesus met at the well. As Jesus began engaging her for a discussion, she began building defensive walls around her as she emphasized that Jews and Samaritans have no dealings. The reality is the root of her defense was not really the fact that He was a Jew and she a Samaritan, but principally because of her past marital experiences with five different men. You can see here that her past experiences became a psychological barrier between her and the word of God. Her experiences affected her personality. Therefore, it is not only important to get to preach to someone, but be very conscious and sensitive to the individual so you can discern or have a clue as to what they might have gone through that may have affected the manner in which they respond to the gospel.

Certain indicators can give you a clue into their personality. They include:

i. **The manner in which the person behaves towards you:** Seeming uninterested, will be a clue he or she could be dealing with something either a physical issue, a past experience, and or psychological one.

ii. **The kind of questions the person interrupts you with**. This is a serious indicator. The questions always point to the areas in which they have been affected.

iii. **How often are the questions coming in.** This could mean the issue may be very particular to them and a point of concern for them.

iv. **Comfort with the answers:** Is the person comfortable with the answers you give to their questions or do they become agitated or start fidgeting even before you fully explain your answer?

v. **Post-response reaction**: How does the person feel after you answer them? Are they excited or they still look disturbed or uncomfortable?

vi. **Openness to further dialogue**: Is the individual still comfortable for further future dialogue on same issue?

vii. **Topic choices**: Is there some topics the individual is not comfortable to hear or talk about?? It could be a good indicator to a hurt in the past which they might have not been completely healed from.

viii. **Emotional reaction**: As you talk, does the person shed tears, or feels broken? This could mean you are hitting the right spot.

These are very important indicators that will definitely influence their response towards you and the gospel. That is why as we minister the gospel to individuals; we must be flexible and not be in a rush to finish saying what we have purposed in our hearts to say. As we talk, we should watch out for feedbacks. These could be simply facial expressions, certain timely postures and gestures, questions, etc. It is great while you are talking, to ask certain key questions that could cause them to open-up more, either to share with you an experience or pain, or whatever had been a concern for them. Failure to do so and just rather go on and on with your sermon could be very ineffective.

A True Evangelistic Message

Though it focuses more on the person of Christ Jesus, yet it is one that is very relative to the individual you are witnessing to. The content of the message is not only what is written in the scriptures, but its presentation must be in a way that will capture aspects of the life of the person. This is because most people become more open to what they can easily relate or identify with. The feedback you get will inspire you as to what else to say, how to drill the message. Once you can perceive that you have touched the sensitive issues of their lives or what they can identify with, based on their response, then shed more light around the issue as you extend to him the call for salvation. That is the Conviction Threshold Point (CTP) - This is the moment within a sermon that an individual is most convicted and can easily make a positive decision with regards to the message.

Every skilled laborer(evangelist) must watch out for this point. This is the moment where the Spirit of conviction grabs the soul of the individual beyond any doubtful question he may want to project. This was the point while Peter was preaching to the people who were mocking the disciples for speaking in tongues on the day of Pentecost, they got convicted and cried for help: ***"Now when they heard this, they were pricked in their heart, and said unto Peter and the rest of the apostles, Men and brethren, what shall we do? Then Peter said unto them, Repent..." Acts 2:37-38 KJV***

Often, this point arrives when the preacher is not yet done with his sermon. The worst thing as an evangelist to do is to continue preaching beyond this point, especially when you are intending to win that soul to the Lord. Else, you could eventually preach them out of conviction. In the story of this Ethiopian eunuch, when he was fully convicted by the preaching of Philip, he then asked Philip what could now prevent him from being baptized. Philip's response was, ***"If only you believe,"*** which he agreed. Hence, Philip immediately baptized him. Then the Holy Ghost raptured Philip to a different place and the eunuch went home rejoicing. You can see here that the Holy Ghost raptured Philip immediately after the conversion of the eunuch. Is to tell us that this was the key point - the Conviction Threshold Point. The result was that the man got saved, and then went home rejoicing. Become sensitive and a skillful harvester for the Lord.

The Conviction Threshold Point

This is a point during the message and preaching of the evangelist to the sinner that the individual gets most convicted. This is the best moment to engage the individual into accepting the Lord Jesus even when the sermon delivery is not yet done. Preaching after this point may drive the individual out of conviction, or some other thing may interrupt and it may become difficult to bring the individual into the CTP again.

The goal of every soul-winner in preaching is not to finish delivering a particular sermon to the unbeliever, but to get the individual to this CTP (the rest will be handled during discipleship). Then he takes advantage of it and lead him to the Lord. So, the soul-winner must be sensitive enough to identify when an individual gets to this point. It may take much longer for others to get to this point, while for others, a story or personal experience can help facilitate them getting faster to the CTP. For this to be feasible, the soul-winner as he preaches, must be very observant for feedbacks, whether verbal or non-verbal.

Tips In Determining the Conviction Threshold Point

Either of these tips will be enough to identify the CTP. In some cases, many of these tips will be portrayed in the feedback of the one you are evangelizing, while in some cases, a few or just one. In either of the cases, it will be enough to ask if they will like to make a commitment for the Lord. If they chose not to, know that they might have been convicted and may just be battling making the decision. They could be needing more time, to which you both could make other appointments. Often, most of them later on in life accepts the Lord, and may testify that they kept hearing the voice of the evangelist weeks, months or even years after. That is the power of conviction *(Ps 62:11).* These tips are:

i. When the individual's focus is totally given without any sign of impatience to listen.

ii. When they are impressed with the answers you give to the questions they pose before you (Acts 8:30-36).

iii. When he comes to the point that he no longer questions just to disagree with the preacher, but listening as he takes deep breaths; insinuating he is now comfortable with what you are saying.

iv. When he expresses positive emotions (smiling, laughing, tears of joy, or words of affirmation) to what you are saying.

v. He may get to narrate an event about their lives in affirmation to your preaching.

vi. When he starts to ask questions about what then should he do.

Be Watchful Against Self-Projection

In as much as your personal experiences could be very useful while witnessing to an individual, ensure it's not merely self-projection. This is because nothing becomes more repulsive than when the person feels you simply being prideful and showing off. Nobody wants to sacrifice their precious time to listen to someone they feel is merely trying to project himself. To ensure your personal testimony is not being received in the wrong way, watch out for the following:

i. Search your heart as to the reason why you want to share it.

ii. How does it fit in with the bigger picture (what you are teaching).

iii. Does it help convince someone to receive the gospel and to believe the Lord Jesus Christ.

iv. When do I call the shots. That is, to what extent do I share a particular experience and what details are necessary? Certain details may mislead your audience from what you intend to communicate.

Personality or Self-Management

The manner in which you present yourself before who you are preaching to matters. Know that as you witness to an individual, especially someone of a high profile, he or she in listening to you is very observant. He can prey on you if he notices that you are a novice at what you are saying. Many people have gone to witness the gospel, and their audience finds it to be an opportunity to argue certain theological concerns with.

No matter who the person you are witnessing to is, never appear to be intimidated. Else, they will use you to practice their little theology on.

No matter who the person you are witnessing to is, never appear to be intimidated. Else, they will use you to practice their little theology on. Paul caution Timothy not to allow himself to be despised because of his youthfulness, rather to show himself as an example to the believers in words, conversation, spirit, faith, and charity *(1 Tim 4:11-12).* This is because the way you present yourself might cause the individual to feel superior over you, hence, hindering effective witnessing. Paul understood this factor properly well and how to get the attention of his listeners. No doubt King Agrippa during Paul's trial said he almost convinced him to be saved within such a short time of him talking. Paul's response was not only to convert him, but also all who hear him *(Acts 26:28-29).*

This means Paul was so efficient at witnessing and was so at the top of his game that within a short time, he drove conviction into Agrippa. The statement Agrippa made to Paul was aimed at intimidating him. But Paul immediately understood that and boldly responded that his intention is not only to get him saved, but with everyone who hears him in this defense. This is so powerful as it makes Agrippa knows Paul is on top of his game and not a novice at what he is doing, but knows exactly what he is up to. No doubt he would have released Paul as he found no fault in him, if not for the fact that he had appealed to see Caesar the emperor at Rome *(Acts 26:32).*

The way you see yourself indeed matters. There was a time in Israel's history as they walked through the wilderness, they had to encounter the Canaanites. The manner in which they looked at themselves with regards to the Canaanites, influenced the way the Canaanites looked at them– as grasshoppers (Num 13:33). Therefore, though self-projection is wrong, yet, never have any inferiority complex whenever you approach someonc. Rather, be courageous, positive, bold, and communicate eloquently while looking at them above their shoulders. It places you in control of the moment as they become submissive to listen to you. Paul says he became all things to all men that by all means he may win some to the Lord *(1 Corinthians 9:19-23).*

Principle 11: You Are Likely Not the First to Approach the Individual

Never think you are the first person to reach a particular individual with the gospel. Even if the individual is in an unreached field, he or she might have heard in one way or the other, or maybe over the radio. So, it is important to know that the person you are going to witness to, some other more strategic and skilled evangelist might have tried preaching to before and did not succeed in converting him. Not because they did an error in the area of witnessing to him. This consciousness is so vital, so you realize it is not by your ability that you will succeed, but by the grace of God. With such understanding, you approach them prayerfully relying totally on the Lord for success. This is where evangelism becomes a spiritual warfare for souls. It must not be taken lightly. Jesus will daily spend hours on the mount in prayers every night for souls, then go out in the day to save them.

Everyone who is involved in evangelizing must realize that there is no other spiritual warfare more powerful than evangelizing. The results of evangelism (whether souls will be won and remained in the faith) will be determined by how much the believer intercedes for them during his prayer moments. It is time to contend for the souls of men (See Mt 12:29, Lk 12:11/Mt 10:19).

Principle 12: Everyone Needs A "Me-Moment!"

Beware a person in pursuit of God also wants a *"Me Moment."* One of the greatest weaknesses of unexperienced evangelists is they want to preach an 'unending gospel.' They do not realize that even when people are excited to listen to the word, they also need time for themselves. They keep winding out time as they preach long messages, thereby getting into irrelevant issues. People want to be accountable for their time and not to be wasted by irrelevant issues. A matured and skilled evangelist will be conscious of the fact that though a person shows the interest to listen, yet, he or she also has other important things to take care of, and he must be respectful of their time. That does not mean that he is like Martha whom Jesus said was busy and worried about unimportant things *(Lk 10:41-42).*

One of the greatest weaknesses of unexperienced evangelists is they want to preach an 'unending gospel.'

It has a demoralizing effect both on you and the meeting with them if they have to let you know that you have taken more time than they were expecting. It influences them psychologically not to be ready for next appointment (if any), and it also discourages you from going next time. Therefore, to avoid being resented or to be told you have spent more time than needed, even when the individual seems to be listening, decide to keep your preaching short and to the point.

> **Keeping the message brief and to the point increases their receptivity and your effectiveness.**

Keeping the message brief and to the point increases their receptivity and your effectiveness. Even if they want you to stay, reschedule a meeting with them for a different day, as you let them know you have other things to attend to. This will prepare them psychologically to always be ready for you as they know you have the habit of being brief and to the point. And they also learn to cherish and respect the time spent with you as they know you had sacrificed certain things just to share with them the word.

This will build respect for you, as they will not become unnecessarily familiar with you to think you have nothing else to do. It helps them to be conscious of the other important things they were sleeping on without realizing. They can then quickly address it without feeling the time spent with you prevented them from accomplishing other things.

QUESTIONS

1. A person social status influences his response to the evangelist. True or False?
2. Who is a delicate person?
3. Who is a biblical example of a delicate person examined in this chapter?
4. Give five indicators that can help you know a person's personality?
5. What will you consider to be a true evangelistic message?
6. What is the conviction threshold point?
7. The conviction threshold point is when the preacher is done with his sermon. True or False?
8. Give five tips in determining the conviction threshold point?
9. What must we watch out for when sharing our personal experiences?
10. What is the most powerful form of spiritual warfare?

CHAPTER 6

ALL PROTOCOLS RESPECTED

Principle 13: Effectiveness and productivity is when wisdom is factored into talent and skill.

I know many may be wondering what does this mean! In every field, whether medical, technology, business, religious, there is a leadership structure. Also, the different aspects surrounding that field must be treated accordingly in keeping with the demanded ethics. For example, visiting a chieftaincy palace in Africa, there is an expected behavior as you get into the palace. Often, there are palace guards who will properly educate you before you are granted audience by the king. They will educate you how to greet him, where not to go, when to stand before the king. All these has to do with the protocol of the environment. Failure to comply, your presence will be seen as an attack on the King's life, and you will be treated accordingly.

Likewise, everyone has their personal protocols surrounding their spaces. To have their attention to preach to them, you need to behave in ways that show honor and respect for them, their present engagements, and all that surrounds them. For example, a person will find it honoring and dignifying if you meet them, and begin by greeting; approaching them in a way that shows respect for whatever they might be engaged in at the moment, appreciating their work and commitment to what they are engaged in, while desiring to speak with them for a little bit so as not to interrupt their commitments. Also demonstrating to them that you are willing to be a little patient for them to get through whatever they are busy with. They will consider that as great honor for them and their time. Most of them would likely halt that which they are engaged in so as to listen to you. This because you valued and respected their space.

Many impatient believers and evangelists may not understand this and its depth. They think because they have showed up, the individual must suspend what they are currently engage in to be able to give them a listening ear. That is rude and a proof that they are yet unskilled in the art of evangelizing. That is the difference between an apprentice evangelist and one who is actually in the office of the evangelist.

The maturity of every leader is seen in his wisdom on how he manages his duties.

The maturity of every leader is seen in his wisdom on how he manages his duties.

The Office of the Evangelist

Office is a position of authority through which a person under an organization executes certain responsibilities. It is not much of a physical space as much as it is a body of responsibilities being channeled in a systematic sequence to achieve a particular objective. Generally speaking, though a person may occupy an office, it may likely take a trained team (formally or informally) to accomplish its responsibilities. This would mean the main person must know how to set the various structures together and define the various responsibilities of the

> **Nothing hinders and breaks a team like disorder and difference in mindsets.**

team members. Leadership skills are demanded if the objectives must be met with perfect harmony amongst team members.

Nothing hinders and breaks a team like disorder and difference in mindsets. So, the goal of every evangelist should be to grow the office of an evangelist by mentoring and coaching other growing up evangelists is realized. This is where common and careless mistakes made by other young growing evangelists have been fully addressed by the one occupying the office. Just as there was the school of the prophets in the days of Elijah, so also there need to be the school of the Evangelists.

Jesus was not only a soul-winner but He also dedicated His time in teaching, training and discipling others to know how to win souls for the Lord. Certain times, He hid Himself from the multitude who were running after Him because He was busy teaching and training His disciples. He did this to guarantee longevity and posterity of the ministry. He did not want to run a ministry that will dissolve with the departure of the founder, but should continue as though the founder Himself was there. As such, He decided to dedicate most of His time in mentoring and coaching the disciples for the continuity of the work that He began. This act of mentoring and coaching others while equipping them for ministry is what Scripture meant when it said about Jesus: ***"And it was He who gave some to be apostles, some to be prophets, and some to be evangelists...to equip the saints for works of ministry and to build up the body of Christ." Eph 4:11-12 BSB.***

Growing Into the Office of An Evangelist

Notice that though the Great Commission has to do principally with evangelism and discipleship, which must be observed by all, not all have been called into the office of the evangelist. Timothy was called into the pastoral ministry, but was commanded by Paul to do the work of an evangelist *(2 Tim 4:5)*. This is worth noting; irrespective of whatever your calling is, doing the work of an evangelist is one of your principal duties: ***"When I say to the wicked person, 'You will surely die,' and you do not warn them or speak out to dissuade them from their evil ways in order to save their life, that wicked person will for their sin, and I will hold you accountable for their blood. But if you do warn the wicked person and they do not turn from their wickedness or from their evil ways, they will die for their sin; but you will have saved yourself." Ezekiel 3:18-19***

Unfortunately, most of those who are called into the office of the evangelist never grow up to attain it. To be called into an office does not automatically get you into the office. Many have the calling of an evangelist and function as one, but have not been able to grow into that office. Growing into the office of your calling is a whole lot. No one sits in an office who is still a novice or an apprentice. It comes with thorough training (formal and informal). It involves exercising the ministry of the evangelist in different settings (including cross-culture), encountering and managing possible challenges that evangelists face, understanding properly the ministry of the evangelist, and principally growing in the grace, gifts, skills of the evangelist. Coupled with all of these, gaining the approval of God into the office of the evangelist.

The office is at a different level and dynamics of ministry. It's a door you have walked into, to take you to the next level of the evangelistic ministry. Here, you are involved in training and coaching fellow evangelists. It has always been God's pattern for people to grow into higher level of responsibilities(offices) in the ministry. It comes depending on how much the Lord can trust you. That is part of what it means by many have been called but few chosen. The same is true for the man who had five talents and brought back ten. The one talent of the man who did nothing was taken and added to his ten; implying more responsibility. John the Apostle was given assignments to write letters to the churches *(Rev 1-3).* It was in deed a mammoth task. After he finished executing the assignment to the seven churches, a special door was opened to him for a more honorable and demanding responsibility: ***"After this I looked, and there before me was a door standing open in heaven. And the voice I had first heard speaking to me like a trumpet said, "Come up here, and I will show you what must take place after this." Rev 4:1***

When Jesus specified taking the gospel to the ends of the earth, you would realize that not every believer is approved of God to take it to that extent. It comes with dedication, devotion, sacrifice, growth and expertise. This is attained by fully executing past assignments from the Lord in the area of evangelism. The Lord also searches the heart of the person to find out the motives and intents of the heart *(Heb 4:12).* Some ministers may seek for connections to nations, and it will take laboring to maintain such the doors, as opposed to the Lord preparing you for those international doors, and opens them for you. Most ministers will eventually get into some schemes and games to maintain it; manipulating people for flight tickets, etc. That does not mean that the door was opened by God, and will never reap the results even if it was God who opened it.

QUESTIONS

1. In evangelizing, never follow the protocol of the environment. True or False?
2. When you go out to evangelize, show respect to what the individual is engaged in. True or False?
3. In evangelizing, do you expect people to immediately give up what they are doing to listen to you or you need to exercise patience?
4. Nothing breaks a team like____________ and difference in__________________.
5. Timothy was called into __________ ministry, but was commanded to ____________.
6. The minister should manipulate people for international doors to be opened. True or False?
7. Most of those who are called into the office of an evangelist, ends up not fully attaining it. True or False?
8. What is some of the responsibility in addition to evangelizing, does an individual who has grown into the office of an evangelist has?
9. How can you know a matured leader?
10. What is one of the differences between an apprentice evangelist and one who has occupied the office?

CHAPTER 7

PERSPECTIVES ABOUT EVANGELISM

Principle 14: If your perspective doesn't line up with biblical worldview and ideals, then you need a mind renewal

What is shared in this chapter is the results from a series of interviews conducted on pastors, Christian individuals, and the general public with regards to the subject of evangelism. Most of these questions have been addressed within this book already. The aim here is to know what people think about evangelism, its importance, and why most believers do not find themselves evangelizing, and so on. Some of their responses may not be accurate or conclusive. The purpose is not accuracy in terms of the truth of what they say, rather it is to showcase sample mindsets with regards to the subject. All these will be very instrumental for the soul-winner to help him or her become more effective in saving lives. Here are the various interviews conducted and the responses:

Why Do Christians Not Evangelize?

This is a very important question because evangelism as popularly said, is the heartbeat of God. Preaching to the lost and making disciples for the Lord is what God wants us to be preoccupied with in our journey in this life. It Is really the command that Jesus left for the church when He was ascending to heaven. The reasons for not evangelizing by many could be either of the following:

Firstly, I believe it is the result of lack of understanding of the importance placed on it by the Scriptures. We need to know as believers that we are the salt of the earth. Christ taught and said we are the salt, which means we are the ones to flavor the world. Not only that we are the light of the world, we are the ones to declare the Goodnews so that light can shine in this world of darkness. But when we don't understand that we are the salt or the light, we then become like salt that has lost its flavor or the light that is hidden under the table. As salt, we savor this world. As such, people can then come to the saving knowledge of Jesus Christ. We ought to declare the Goodnews, which is the light of the Gospel.

Secondly, people live in fear of sharing their faith. The Bible makes us to understand that God has not given us the spirit of fear, but of boldness, love, and a sound mind. Boldness is of the essence if we will declare the word of God. God being for us is assurance that no one can succeed in their cunning devices against us *(Rom 8:31).*

According to the Scriptures in view of the Great Commission, we are told that God's manifest presence will be with us when we go to declare the Goodnews of the Kingdom of God to the lost. They will come to the saving knowledge of Jesus, and God will back our ministry with signs and wonders. Lack of this understanding of Scriptures keeps believers within the four walls of the church, as the church leaders just keep on doing maintenance instead of reaching out to a dying world.

Thirdly, some people tend to lead a defeated life. A believer that lives a defeated life is not bold enough to go into the world of darkness and preach the Gospel. The world was just from celebrating Easter. During the time of Easter, we know the story of the two disciples that left Jerusalem very discouraged, and on their way to Emmaus, Christ intercepted them *(Lk 24:13-32).* They were discouraged because of the death and burial of Christ, to the extent that when Christ resurrected, they didn't even know. And when Christ intercepted them, they got stirred up and their eyes were opened. Hence, they became fired up to go preach the Gospel. So, a life of defeat is a life that is less optimal, not really celebrating the goodness of God, and unable to declare the Goodnews to the world. It is my prayer that believers will be bold to speak God's word.

Fourthly, a lack of compassion. If we understood that those who die in sin without the knowledge of the Lord Jesus Christ are eternally lost, our hearts will be triggered to reach them.

These are the major reasons I can share why people do not evangelize.

Rev Dr. Kenneth Tah

PHD Finance and Professor of Finance at Mercer University

Lead Pastor at Jubilee Full Gospel Church in Warner Robins

Superintendent for The Full Gospel Ministers USA.

What was your greatest regret evangelizing? How did you overcome it?

Evangelizing and not being able to follow-up with the persons, nor getting their contact information to ensure they grow with the Lord. Another great challenge and regrets are the fact that when I began evangelizing as a younger person, I thought I had to memorize certain phrases in order to be able to get my listeners saved. I so much relied on my head knowledge about the path to get someone to Jesus. Unfortunately, I would forget periodically some of the crammed information, and my listeners would look at me stocked, and they would walk away. I would feel embarrassed of misrepresenting Christ because I had not yet had a proper training to help me to be effective. I realized I was considering evangelism as not a very serious thing to sacrifice my time and finances to attend a formal training. I had to eventually enroll in a training institute that gave me all the training on the subject that I needed. The training also helped me build a relationship with the Lord and His word.

Now, having grown in the Lord and having had proper training on the subject, I share the gospel from a meet-my-friend perspective; I tell people I would like to introduce them to a friend, who is both Lord and Savior, and who will bring them to freedom as He grants those who believes, eternal life. When they get saved, I get their contact details to ensure they get plugged in a local church for subsequent discipleship and fellowship.

Evangelist Justin Bell

Senior Pastor

Greater Glory World Ministries, USA

What Will Preserve One's Fire For Evangelism?

1. Walk with the Holy Spirit daily.
2. Pray in the Spirit and always carry His fire.
3. Live an empowered Holy Spirit driven lifestyle of a soul winner.
4. Be a student of the Word.
5. Love God and love people passionately.

Pastor Rylance Mbu

Planetshakers Church, Cape Town, RSA.

Why Many Who Travelled Abroad Lost Their Passion for Evangelism

Why are people not concerned about Evangelism To my opinion, the first reason people are not concerned about Evangelism is because they don't make it a lifestyle. If something has become your lifestyle, you do it without thinking because it reflects your personality. If we don't consciously choose to make Evangelism a lifestyle, we will rarely think of evangelizing to others. Secondly, the fear of rejection, that is those you intend to evangelize not willing to either listen or to accept the message, can also be another reason why many are not concerned about evangelizing. Thirdly, the lack of the passion for evangelism is something that causes many not to desire making it a lifestyle. We have to recognize the fact that we are in a relationship with Jesus Christ today because somebody was courageous enough to evangelized us. Let us reciprocate that love by sharing Christ's love to others. Hence, becoming a vessel through which His love will flow through to others. We are accountable for those we choose not to share Christ's love with.

Mr Yango Collins,

Masters in Electrical Engineering

Houston Texas.

Why Do Many Immigrants Loss Their Passion For Evangelism, And How Can It Be Corrected?

A victorious Christian life with regards to evangelism can only be sustained through a consistent prayer life. Many immigrants, especially from Africa, had their Christian experience sustained through their consistent prayer life. Many prior to travelling abroad, could seek the Lord and be in His presence to be strengthened for hours daily. However, when they travel abroad, they are faced with the challenges of a new culture that is likely fast paced. Many have given up the time set aside for prayers and waiting on God and rather have gone after more jobs to enable them to ease the financial pressure. Having these many jobs to keep up with financial responsibilities is not a bad thing. However, it has come at the expense of their passion for evangelism.

To correct this negative reversal, it will be very necessary to consider the place of prayer in our Christian walk with the Lord, and go back to the place of prayer and waiting on the Lord. The passion for soul winning is spiritual and is being given birth to by the spirit of God. This will reawaken the individual spiritually and will cause him to restructure his schedule in a way that permits him to still evangelize irrespective of the jobs.

Pastor Nkrumah Ndingha,

Canada

What Will You Consider as a Successful Evangelism?

To begin with, the gospel is a seed, and every time we plant seeds, there could be different outcomes based on the climate and environment. The seed can either grow or dies. The Most significant seed, is the seed of the gospel. It never dies. Like a mustard seed, if you define it by its size, you would probably be mistaken, as its outcome is phenomenal. This is same with the seed of the gospel with regards to Evangelism. I will therefore say, successful evangelism is not just reaching out to a soul or an individual, but bringing them to a place of making a heart commitment to becoming a disciple of the Lord Jesus Christ. Plucking them into a forum for discipleship and follow-up is the way to go. Thanks.

Pastor Valery Njume

Senior Pastor: Salvation City Ministries, Irving Texas

What Was Your Greatest Fear About Evangelizing

Evangelism to me was a very challenging command from the Lord. My fear I would guess was different from others, because I have always been outgoing and extroverted. I have never been afraid of approaching people, irrespective of whether I knew them or not. So, my fear was more on the side of what the person would do with the message that I share with him or her. I was indeed scared if they will not accept, receive, or commit themselves to a gospel that I considered to be life or death situation. Because of that, the thought of evangelizing became very challenging to me, as I would ponder if it was even worth taking the gospel to people, if they only had to reject it. So my fear was about the end result.

At moment, I would say I am still in the process of overcoming the fear. But I realize that the only way to overcome it, is to go out and evangelize and do not bother about the result. For it is the role of the Holy Spirit to bring the people into conviction and repentance.

Pastor Luis(Venezuelan)

Associate Pastor at Antioch Church, Dallas, TX.

What Has Been Your Experience Evangelizing?

I am a citizen from Bangladesh, and have lived there all my life. It has a dense population, of which approximately 91% are Muslims and 0.30% Christians. As a youth and member of my Church family, I have been privileged to attend different Christian training programs, seminars, youth camps, etc. These have helped me to develop myself for a more effective Christian service, especially evangelizing.

Unfortunately, according to the perspective of the culture of Bangladesh, I haven't attained the age that permits people to listen to me preach the gospel. That makes evangelizing for me very difficult. Also, since the Muslims are the vast majority, often they will not want to listen aswell. They really do not like to hear much about Jesus, though they love to engage in discussions in which they want to find about about how many different Christian feasts such as Chritmas are there, the reason why some Christians do not drink alcohol, why Christians do not offer sacrifices, and much more. Whenever I try to talk about Jesus, they would just laugh at me and make a fun of the whole discussion, as they immediately switch making appraisals to Mohammed.

I remember when I was in Grade 11, in College, one of my Business Studies teachers asked me why I believe that Jesus Christ is the Son of God. I replied that because the Holy Bible says so. He made a mockery of me saying how could that be possible. But because in our culture, it is considered disrespectful whether in class or out of class for a student to argue with her teacher, so that made it difficult for me to really explain that to him. So I would normally share mostly with my classmates, even while in the University. Many of them love hearing stories about Jesus if we consider Him as a prophet and not the Savior. The more I evangelized, the more I realized I need more knowledge about the gospel to be effective. As such, I dedicated more time daily in studying the Holy Bible, regularly attending family prayer moments. All these have so impacted my life, helped me in properly responding to questions about the faith whenever I am being asked, changed my perspective of life, how I see myself and relate with Christ.

Smita Hansda(Age 32)

Bangladesh Lutheran Church

Youth Volunteer

How to use Digital Outreach to Advance the Gospel

We live in a digital world. With the advancement of technology, people's lifestyle has become increasingly reliant on digital assets; phones, tablets, computers, all connected to the internet. According to datareportal.com, a total of 5.30 billion people around the world use the internet today–equivalent to 63.1 percent of the world's total population.

Globally the number of internet users increased from only 413 million in 2000 to over 3.4 billion in 2016. The one-billion barrier was crossed in 2005. Every day over the past 5 years, an average of 640,000 people went online for the first time.

Jesus said go into all the world (And he said unto them, Go ye into all the world, and preach the gospel to every creature. Mark 16:15) – thanks to that fact, digital outreach is a major consideration to advance the gospel.

The right Digital Outreach training will help individuals, groups, churches or organization;

- Generate more traffic and leads and close more leads; you'll be able to close the gap between outreach and conversion, via principles and techniques in lead management, content marketing, and growth hacking, to attract more qualified leads, and close the outreach-conversion loop.
- Identify the Right Marketing Channels for Their Needs; you'll be able to choose the right technology that fits the outreach goals, needs or targets, to get you the best returns for the least possible effort.
- Prove the Returns on Digital Outreach to encourage more investments from you, your church, partners-donors-sponsors: you'll be able to take advantage of a more data driven digital outreach, so you can know where to spend, and how much to spend on each channel, based on data, not conjecture.

- Get Hands-on experience on a plethora of tools and technologies for digital outreach; Wordpress, Google Ads, Social Media Marketing (Facebook Advertising, Instagram, Twitter, Hootsuite, Snapchat) MailChimp, Moz, Email Marketing (Google My Business), Video Marketing (Youtube), Search Engine Marketing (Search Engine Optimization (SEO) and Search Engine Advertising (SEA)-) and much more.
- Take the lead in Digital Presence: through proper digital outreach training individuals, churches, and organizations, can take the lead in digital presence and outreach by having mastering in SEO and Content Marketing to Search and Facebook Advertising, web development, with creative, analytical and technical skills, which are valuable assets to furtherance of digital outreach.

Dr. Coach Achu Gustave (AEC-Sr)

Corporate Development Strategist,

Cyber Strategist/Instructor,

CSCU-CEH-CHFI-CEI

As a pastor, how would you encourage Christians to evangelize.

It will be by showing them the importance of evangelism . Make them know they need to evangelize because:

1) Christ commanded it (Matt 28:18-20).
2) Jesus Christ is the only way of salvation (Jn 14:6)
3) Christ died for the world (Jn 3:16)
4) Churches that are not intentional about evangelism become weak.
5) Churches tend to have real unnecessary problems when they fail to grow.
6) Evangelistic Christians actually grow stronger in faith and become better disciples of Christ.
7) Teach the Christians that God's heartbeat is the salvation of souls.

1. 8)The Apostles also commanded believers to evangelize (2 Tim 4:2-5)

8) Through evangelism many people would be encouraged because the gospel is good news.
9) Evangelism is an opportunity to work with God and for God (Lk 10:2).

2. 11)It proves our love for Jesus Christ (Jn 15:12-14).
3. 12) Evangelism opens the door for healings, miracles (Lk 10:19)

4. 13) Evangelism is the fruit of righteousness (Prov 11:30)

REV ERIC FON FORTU

NATIONAL EVANGELIST

THE APOSTOLIC CHURCH CAMEROON

CHAPTER 8

THE SOUL-WINNERS' LIBRARY

Principle 15: If You Are Not Resourceful, You Are Ineffective

This chapter is aimed at helping the believer who is wondering which scriptures to share from when he or she goes out evangelizing. These scriptures have been grouped to help facilitate the process. It gives clarity to the group of scriptures needed based on what the one evangelizing is addressing. Though the entire Bible is full of possible scriptures for evangelism, these few are those that are commonly used.

Efficiency is the result of capacity building, which is directly proportionate to the acquisition of knowledge.

I would encourage every believer to read through and memorize all these scriptures. It will enrich your evangelistic life with resourceful Scriptures in ways that you cannot imagine.

Efficiency is the result of capacity building, which is directly proportionate to the acquisition of knowledge. God bless you for desiring to become a soul-winner.

I. Consequences of Sin

Isaiah 59:2 (ESV) But your iniquities have made a separation between you and your God, and your sins have hidden his face from you so that he does not hear.

Romans 3:23 (ESV) For all have sinned and fall short of the glory of God.

Romans 6:23 (ESV) For the wages of sin is death, but the free gift of God is eternal life in Christ Jesus our Lord.

Isaiah 53:6 (ESV) All we like sheep have gone astray; we have turned—every one—to his own way; and the Lord has laid on him the iniquity of us all.

Hebrews 9:27 (ESV) And just as it is appointed for man to die once, and after that comes judgment,

John 10:10 (ESV) The thief comes only to steal and kill and destroy. I came that they may have life and have it abundantly.

Proverbs 18:21 (ESV) Death and life are in the power of the tongue, and those who love it will eat its fruits.

II. Christ Sacrificial Work

Peter 2:24 (ESV) He himself bore our sins in his body on the tree, that we might die to sin and live to righteousness. By his wounds you have been healed.

Isaiah 53:5 (ESV) But he was pierced for our transgressions; he was crushed for our iniquities; upon him was the chastisement that brought us peace, and with his wounds we are healed.

Isaiah 53:1-6 (ESV) Who has believed what he has heard from us? And to whom has the arm of the Lord been revealed? For he grew up before him like a young plant, and like a root out of dry ground; he had no form or majesty that we should look at him, and no beauty that we should desire him. He was despised and rejected by men, a man of sorrows and acquainted with grief; and as one from whom men hide their faces he was despised, and we esteemed him not. Surely he has borne our griefs and carried our sorrows; yet we esteemed him stricken, smitten by God, and afflicted. But he was pierced for our transgressions; he was crushed for our iniquities; upon him was the chastisement that brought us peace, and with his wounds we are healed. All we like sheep have gone astray; we have turned—every one—to his own way; and the Lord has laid on him the iniquity of us all.

Romans 1:16 (ESV) For I am not ashamed of the gospel, for it is the power of God for salvation to everyone who believes, to the Jew first and also to the Greek.

III. GOD'S LOVE FOR SINNERS

John 3:16 (ESV) For God so loved the world, that he gave his only Son, that whoever believes in him should not perish but have eternal life.

Luke 19:10 (ESV) For the Son of Man came to seek and to save the lost.

Romans 5:8 (ESV) But God shows his love for us in that while we were still sinners, Christ died for us.

Revelations 3:20 (ESV) Behold, I stand at the door and knock. If anyone hears my voice and opens the door, I will come in to him and eat with him, and he with me.

John 10:10 (ESV) The thief comes only to steal and kill and destroy. I came that they may have life and have it abundantly.

John 6:51 (ESV) I am the living bread that came from heaven. If anyone eats of this bread, he will live forever. And the bread that I will give for the life of the world is my flesh."

John 4:8-10 (ESV) (For his disciples had gone away into the city to buy food.) The Samaritan woman said to him, ***"How is it that you, a Jew, ask for a drink from me, a woman of Samaria?"*** (For Jews have no dealings with Samaritans.) Jesus answered her, ***"If you knew the gift of God, and who it is that is saying to you, 'Give me a drink,' you would have asked him, and he would have given you living water."***

IV. Our Responsibility to Receive Salvation

Isaiah 55:7 (ESV) Let the wicked forsake his way, and the unrighteous man his thoughts; let him return to the Lord, that he may have compassion on him, and to our God, for he will abundantly pardon.

1 John 1:9 (ESV) If we confess our sins, he is faithful and just to forgive us our sins and to cleanse us from all unrighteousness.

Isaiah 1:18 (ESV) Come now, let us reason together, says the Lord: though your sins are like scarlet, they shall be as white as snow; though they are red like crimson, they shall become like wool.

2 Corinthians 6:2 (ESV) For he says, ***"In a favorable time I listened to you, and in a day of salvation I have helped you."*** Behold, now is the favorable time; behold, now is the day of salvation.

Revelations 3:20 (ESV) Behold, I stand at the door and knock. If anyone hears my voice and opens the door, I will come in to him and eat with him, and he with me.

Romans 10:9 (ESV) Because, if you confess with your mouth that Jesus is Lord and believe in your heart that God raised him from the dead, you will be saved.

Romans 10:13 (ESV) For everyone who calls on the name of the Lord will be saved.

Matthew 22:37-38 (ESV) And he said to him, ***"You shall love the Lord your God with all your heart and with all your soul and with all your mind. This is the great and first commandment."***

Acts 2:21 (ESV) And it shall come to pass that everyone who calls upon the name of the Lord shall be saved.'

John 3:36 (ESV) Whoever believes in the Son has eternal life; whoever does not obey the Son shall not see life, but the wrath of God remains on him.

Acts 16:31 (ESV) And they said, ***"Believe in the Lord Jesus, and you will be saved, you and your household."***

V. Christ The Solution for the Sinner

Revelations 21:1-6 (ESV) Then I saw a new heaven and a new earth, for the first heaven and the first earth had passed away, and the sea was no more. And I saw the holy city, new Jerusalem, coming down out of heaven from God, prepared as a bride adorned for her husband. And I heard a loud voice from the throne saying, ***"Behold, the dwelling place of God is with man. He will dwell with them, and they will be his people,***

and God himself will be with them as their God. He will wipe away every tear from their eyes, and death shall be no more, neither shall there be mourning, nor crying, nor pain anymore, for the former things have passed away." And he who was seated on the throne said, ***"Behold, I am making all things new."*** Also he said, ***"Write this down, for these words are trustworthy and true."*** And he said to me, "It is done! I am the Alpha and the Omega, the beginning and the end. To the thirsty I will give from the spring of the water of life without payment.

Revelations 12:11 (KJV) And they overcame him by the blood of the lamb, and by the word of their testimony; and they loved not their lives unto the death.

Acts 4:12 (ESV) And there is salvation in no one else, for there is no other name under heaven given among men by which we must be saved.

Matthew 10:28 (ESV) And do not fear those who kill the body but cannot kill the soul. Rather fear him who can destroy both soul and body in hell.

1 Peter 3:18 (ESV) For Christ also suffered once for sins, the righteous for the unrighteous, that he might bring us to God, being put to death in the flesh but made alive in the spirit.

2 Corinthians 5:21 (ESV) For our sake he made him to be sin who knew no sin, so that in him we might become the righteousness of God.

John 14:6 (ESV) Jesus said to him, ***"I am the way, and the truth, and the life. No one comes to the Father except through me."***

Psalm 107:6 (KJV) Then they cried unto the LORD in their trouble, [and] he delivered them out of their distresses.

Psalm 34:17 (KJV) The righteous cry, and the LORD heareth, and delivereth them out of all their troubles.

Psalm 50:15 (KJV) And call upon me in the day of trouble: I will deliver thee, and thou shalt glorify me.

VI. GOD'S EXPECTATION FOR US

Leviticus 19:2 (ESV) Speak to all the congregation of the people of Israel and say to them, You shall be holy, for I the Lord your God am holy

1 John 3:4-10 (ESV) Everyone who makes a practice of sinning also practices lawlessness; sin is lawlessness. You know that he appeared in order to take away sins, and in him there is no sin. No one who abides in him keeps on sinning; no one who keeps on sinning has either seen him or known him. Little children, let no one deceive you. Whoever practices righteousness is righteous, as he is righteous. Whoever makes a practice of sinning is of the devil, for the devil has been sinning from the beginning. The reason the Son of God appeared was to destroy the works of the devil. No one born of God makes a practice of sinning, for God's seed abides in him; and he cannot keep on sinning, because he has been born of God. By this it is evident who are the children of God, and who are the children of the devil: whoever does not practice righteousness is not of God, nor is the one who does not love his brother.

Psalm 1:1-6 (ESV) Blessed is the man who walks not in the counsel of the wicked, nor stands in the way of sinners, nor sits in the seat of scoffers; but his delight is in the law of the Lord, and on his law he meditates day and night. He is like a tree planted by streams of water that yields its fruit in its season, and its leaf does not wither. In all that he does, he prospers. The wicked are not so, but are like chaff that the wind drives away. Therefore the wicked will not stand in the judgment, nor sinners in the congregation of the righteous; for the Lord knows the way of the righteous, but the way of the wicked will perish.

Proverbs 3:5-8 (ESV) Trust in the LORD with all your heart, and do not lean on your own understanding. In all your ways acknowledge him, and he will make straight your paths. Be not wise in your own eyes; fear the LORD, and turn away from evil. It will be healing to your flesh and refreshment to your bones.

John 4:23-24 (ESV) But the hour is coming, and is now here, when the true worshipers will worship the Father in spirit and truth, for the Father is seeking such people to worship him. God is spirit, and those who worship him must worship in spirit and truth."

VII. The Awesomeness of God

Psalm 19:1 (ESV) The heavens declare the glory of God, and the sky above proclaims his handiwork.

Revelations 4:11 (ESV) Worthy are you, our Lord and God, to receive glory and honor and power, for you created all things, and by your will they existed and were created.

John 5:24 (ESV) Truly, truly, I say to you, whoever hears my word and believes him who sent me has eternal life. He does not come into judgment, but has passed from death to life.

Psalm 34:17 (KJV) The righteous cry, and the LORD heareth, and delivereth them out of all their troubles.

1 John 3:1-3 (ESV) See what kind of love the Father has given to us, that we should be called children of God; and so we are. The reason why the world does not know us is that it did not know him. Beloved, we are God's children now, and what we will be has not yet appeared; but we know that when he appears we shall be like him, because we shall see him as he is. And everyone who thus hopes in him purifies himself as he is pure.

Numbers 23:19 (KJV) God is not a man, that he should lie; neither the son of man, that he should repent: hath he said, and shall he not do it? or hath he spoken, and shall he not make it good?

Psalm 89:34 (KJV) My covenant will I not break nor alter the thing that is gone out of my lips.

Isaiah 55:11 (KJV) so shall my word be that goes out from my mouth; it shall not return to me empty, but it shall accomplish that which I purpose, and shall succeed in the thing for which I sent it.

VIII. Consequences Of Rejecting the Gospel

John 3:36 (ESV) Whoever believes in the Son has eternal life; whoever does not obey the Son shall not see life, but the wrath of God remains on him.

John 3:16-18 (ESV) For God so loved the world,[a] that he gave his only Son, that whoever believes in him should not perish but have eternal life. For God did not send his Son into the world to condemn the world, but in order that the world might be saved through him. Whoever believes in him is not condemned, but whoever does not believe is condemned already, because he has not believed in the name of the only Son of God.

Luke 13:3 (ESV) No, I tell you; but unless you repent, you will all likewise perish.

IX. The Beauty and Assurance of Accepting the Gospel

John 1:12 (ESV) But to all who did receive him, who believed in his name, he gave the right to become children of God.

Matthew 11:28 (ESV) Come to me, all who labor and are heavy laden, and I will give you rest.

Ephesians 2:8-9 (ESV) For by grace you have been saved through faith. And this is not your own doing; it is the gift of God, not a result of works, so that no one may boast.

John 6:37 (ESV) All that the Father gives me will come to me, and whoever comes to me I will never cast out.

1 John 5:12-13 (ESV) Whoever has the Son has life; whoever does not have the Son of God does not have life. I write these things to you who believe in the name of the Son of God, that you may know that you have eternal life.

Romans 8:16 (ESV) The Spirit himself bears witness with our spirit that we are children of God.

2 Corinthians 5:17 (ESV) Therefore, if anyone is in Christ, he is a new creation. The old has passed away; behold, the new has come.

Romans 8:1-2 (ESV) There is therefore now no condemnation for those who are in Christ Jesus. For the law of the Spirit of life has set you free in Christ Jesus from the law of sin and death.

Other book titles of Dr. Willibroad W. Ticha

-The Journey

-Cultivating the Spirit of Leadership

-The Life and Ministry of Jesus (The Standard for Excellence In Ministry and Leadership)

-The Battle of the Eye

-Dealing With The Esau Syndrome, Killer of Destinies

-Understanding and Interpreting Dreams and Visions

-Reclaiming Yourself from Emotional Trauma

-Fatherhood (The Peak of Leadership)

-Recovering Your Anointing

-Uncovering Misconceptions and Understanding the Truth on Spiritual Warfare.

-The Man Approved by God

For more information on these or other books by Dr Willibroad Ticha, contact our office on:

Email: gospelheroes18@gmail.com

YOUTUBE

Please subscribe to our YouTube channel and hit the notification button for uplifting teachings on how to identify your purpose and to soar to greater heights in leadership:

YouTube:

GospelHeroes TV

INSTAGRAM

Please subscribe also to our instagram: GospelHeroesTV

FACEBOOK

Please follow us on Facebook at: Dr. Willibroad

OUR MENTORSHIP PROGRAM

To enroll into our mentorship program(Gospel Heroes Commission International) so as to become a cutting-edge leader, of the following:

-Website and register: www.tichawillibroad.com/ghci

-Send us an email to: gospelheroes18@gmail.com

EDITOR DORCA

I have enjoyed reading this book. As one involved in ministry and missions, I have found it practical and in tune with the dynamics of the missionary field. Anyone who reads it will find just as useful in practice as it is sensible in theory. It is also simple, cutting to the point. Everyone who desires to be an effective soul winner needs to read this manual. Good work and God bless.

Pastors and Leaders Seminar, Monrovia - Liberia, 2020

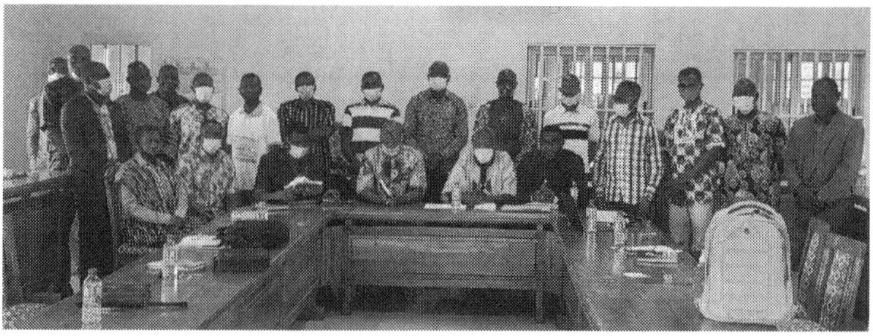

Key Church leaders from the different pastoral associations Togo

Seminar with Pastors and Leaders, Lome - Togo, 2020

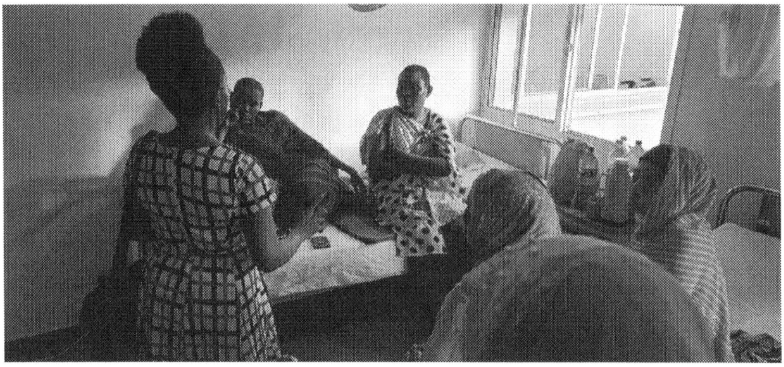

Hospital Evangelism Dar es Salaam - Tanzania

Preaching to my soccer team mates, Denton TX, 2022

Park Evangelism with Papa Dennis and New Zealand team, Dallas TX, 2022

Street Evangelism

Evangelizing and met with these believers

Clarification about the existence of God

Street Evangelism in Johannesburg 2016

Evangelizing infront of the store

Muslims also need Jesus

Evangelizing becomes lively

GospelHeroes Leaders Conference Dallas June 2022

Setting the Church on Fire in Antananarivo-Madagascar

Leading Politicians To Christ

After four days retreating by river in Little Elm TX, a storm broke my tent.

Orphans in Republic of Benin

Leaders Conference and praying for Students of CFNI

Teaching Leaders igniting passion for the Great Commission

Held her to receive the gospel before road trip.

Evangelizing and Praying for political candidates

Street Evangelism

Street Evangelism

Street Evangelism

Street Evangelism

Street Evangelism

Street Evangelism

Street Evangelism

Training hospital chaplains in Africa

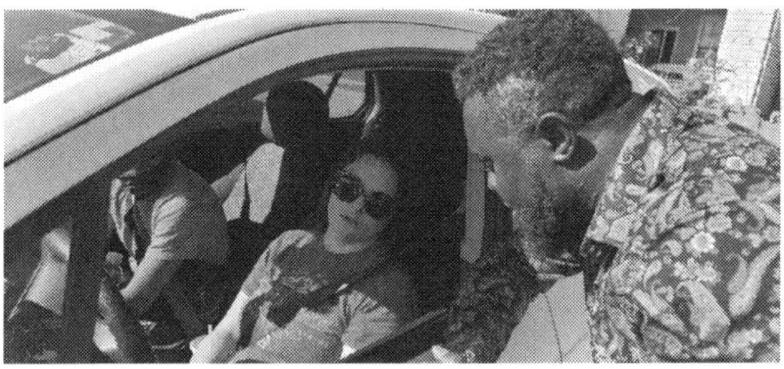

Evangelism

Strategic meeting with key leaders - Liberia

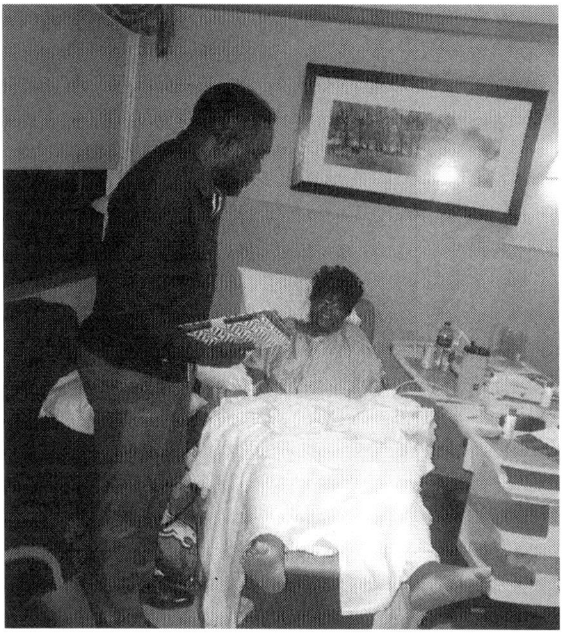

Hospital Evangelism Denver - Colorado

Ministering to Baptist Leaders Denton Texas

Madagascar on Fire

Madagascar on Fire

Made in the USA
Middletown, DE
04 January 2025

68243868R00085